Firms Afloat and Firms Adrift

Hungarian Industry and the Economic Transition

Josef C. Brada
Inderjit Singh
Adám Török

Routledge
Taylor & Francis Group
LONDON AND NEW YORK

First published 1994 by M.E. Sharpe

Published 2015 by Routledge
2 Park Square, Milton Park, Abingdon, Oxon OX14 4RN
711 Third Avenue, New York, NY 10017, USA

Routledge is an imprint of the Taylor & Francis Group, an informa business

Library of Congress Cataloging-in-Publication Data

Brada, Josef C., 1942–
Firms afloat and firms adrift: Hungarian industry and the economic transition / Josef C. Brada, Inderjit Singh, and Ádám Török.
p. cm.
Includes bibliographical references and index.
ISBN 1-56324-320-2 (alk. paper)
1. Hungary—Industries. 2. Hungary—Economic conditions—1989–
I. Singh, Inderjit, 1941– . II. Török, Ádám. III. Title.
HC300.282.B73 1993
338.09439—dc20 93-48903
CIP

ISBN 13: 9781563243202 (pbk)

Firms Afloat and Firms Adrift
is the first volume in the series

MICROECONOMICS OF TRANSITION ECONOMIES

Series editor: JOSEF C. BRADA

Contents

List of Tables

About the Authors

Josef C. Brada was born in Prague, Czechoslovakia, and educated at Tufts University and the University of Minnesota. He has taught at Ohio State University and New York University and has held visiting positions at Stanford University and the Catholic University of Leuven. Professor Brada is the editor of the *Journal of Comparative Economics* and *Eastern European Economics*. He has served as a consultant to the OECD, the World Bank, and the governments of the United States and Czechoslovakia. He is currently Professor of Economics at Arizona State University.

Inderjit Singh holds an MBA and a Ph.D. in Economics from the University of Wisconsin. He is currently Lead Economist in the Transition and Macro Adjustment Division of the Policy Research Department in the World Bank. His extensive career at the World Bank, where he has worked since 1975, included assignments in the China Department, the South Asia Projects Department, and the Office of the Regional Vice-President for Eastern Africa, among others. Prior to the World Bank, he was Associate Professor of Economics at Ohio State University. He has published many articles in professional journals and has authored and edited several books. His current research includes projects on industrial adjustments in China, Eastern Europe, and the former Soviet Union.

Adám Török studied in Budapest, Hungary, and Nancy, France, and earned his Ph.D. in International Economics from the Hungarian Academy of Sciences in 1985. He has been the Director of the Research Institute of Industrial Economics of the Hungarian Academy of Sciences since 1990. The author of three books and more than seventy articles, Dr. Török has lectured at several universities and the research institutions of more than twenty countries of Europe, North America, Latin America, Africa, and Asia. His research topics include international trade, privatization, and industrial economics in the transition. He has advised several Hungarian governmental agencies and firms on privatization and management issues.

Introduction

The countries of Eastern Europe and the former Soviet Union are engaged in the transformation of their economies, away from central planning and social ownership of the means of production and toward the use of the market to allocate resources and private ownership to provide effective stewardship over productive assets. The success of this transition depends to a large extent on developments in the industrial sector of these countries because industry is the largest employer and produces the largest share of output in their economies. Moreover, it is the success of the industrial sector in increasing productivity, restructuring production, and penetrating Western markets that will, to a great extent, determine the speed of transition and the social and economic costs that will have to be borne by these societies. It can be argued that it is in the industrial sector of these economies that the greatest distortions and shortcomings in resource allocation and managerial efficiency are to be found, the result of both mistaken domestic policies and the distorting effects of integration within the framework of the Council for Mutual Economic Assistance (CMEA).

The crucial role of the industrial sector is evident in the focus of policy makers on reforming and privatizing industry and in seeking out foreign investors and technology. At the same time, the industrial sector of the East European countries has had to absorb a series of shocks that have exacerbated the historical burdens placed on it by its communist past. On the domestic front, the demand for industrial output has been reduced in a number of ways. Price liberalization has led to outbursts of inflation, and although inflation has subsided in Czechoslovakia, Hungary, and Poland, real wages, and thus purchasing power and wealth, have declined. At the same time, relative prices of food and other basic consumer goods have risen with the elimination of consumption subsidies. As a result, because the demand for necessities is relatively inelastic, the share of household budgets devoted to purchases of industrial goods came under pressure. Tight domestic monetary and fiscal policies, combined with a slump in consumer demand and uncertainty about the future both in terms of wholesale changes in ownership and management and in terms of restructuring, have served to reduce investment sharply, thus reducing demand for machinery and equipment as well as for construction activity.

External shocks have also taken their toll. The collapse of CMEA trade, and particularly of the import demand of the USSR, had an incalculable effect on East European industry, some of whose sectors were almost totally dependent on the Soviet market. At the same time, as these countries began their reorientation toward the West, the rapid liberalization of their trade regimes brought a wave of new competition for East European industry as Western goods were free to enter East European markets.

Much of this story, including the effects of past legacies and the transition policies as well as of the temporary external shocks, is told by the aggregate data on industrial output, employment, and prices. In Czechoslovakia, industrial output fell by 3.5 percent in 1990 and then by 24.7 percent in 1991 under the double impact of the "big-bang" reform of January 1, 1991, and the collapse of exports to the USSR. In 1992 it fell by another 11 percent, although by the last two quarters the decline had been arrested and evidence of output growth began to appear. In Poland, the "big bang" of January 1, 1990, led to a decline of 14.2 percent in that year's industrial output, and the following year it fell by another 11.9 percent as exports to the USSR dried up. In 1992 there was no decline in industrial output, and, as in Czechoslovakia, signs of an upswing in industrial production were evident. In Hungary, industrial production declined steadily, falling 9.6 percent in 1990, 19.1 percent in 1991, and 10.4 percent in 1992. Interestingly enough, Hungary had no "big-bang" reform comparable to those of the other countries, although it shared with them the shock of the collapse of exports to the USSR; yet it suffered a decline in industrial output of comparable magnitude. Employment declines were everywhere less than the losses in output, but in all countries save the Czech Republic they exceeded 10 percent by 1992, having started from zero in 1989. The Czech Republic's unemployment level peaked at 4.1 percent in 1991, and in 1992 it was down to 2.1 percent. Inflation in Czechoslovakia and Poland peaked in the years of the "big bang," reaching 586 percent in Poland in 1990 and 58 percent in Czechoslovakia in 1991. It subsided rapidly thereafter, falling to 70 and 40 percent in the two following years in Poland and to 11 percent in Czechoslovakia in 1992. In Hungary, there was no "big-bang" price reform, and inflation continued at a moderate rate, rising from 28 percent in 1990 to 35 percent in 1991 and then falling to 21 percent in 1992.

Yet these aggregates reveal only part of the story. The other part cannot be expressed in numbers, because it is the human story of enterprise managers and workers attempting to deal with the unfolding events. Every firm in Eastern Europe is being forced to reassess its competitive strengths, its strategy for survival, its organization, and its role in the broader world economy. It is the outcomes of these individual decisions that will drive the trend of industrial output in future years.

This book uses two approaches in order to give a detailed portrait of Hungarian industry in the context of a sweeping transition in the political and economic system of the country. The first approach is relatively broad: basic indicators of macrolevel industrial performance are analyzed first for the 1980s and then, after a policy analysis for the same decade, for the transition years 1988–91. Exhaustive statistical material is provided to support the performance analysis as well as to help understand the policy assessment. Macropolicy issues influencing industrial development are also discussed. First we provide analyses of the policy issues of the 1980s that had the greatest relevance for industry, with a majority of these issues being related to the economic reform. It has to be seen that some of these topics—price reform, for example—have already lost their relevance. The analysis of the pre-1989 period is important not so much for the economic results obtained during that time as for the economic system that was created in Hungary and the consequences that unique economic system had for reform in the subsequent period. As we shall argue, the reform measures of the pre-1989 period were conceptually flawed and ineffective when judged from the standpoint of decisive improvements in economic performance. Yet they created an economic milieu that included considerable independence for state firms, a nascent private sector, and a certain comfort with non-*dirigiste* methods of influencing economic activity that permitted post-1989 policy makers to proceed in a way that would have been impossible in Czechoslovakia or Poland.

For the period after 1989, we take a different approach. We focus on the options of industrial policy in the new economic environment. This implies that reform has completely disappeared from the agenda due to the very fast changes of the political and economic scene in the country and that industrial policy has to be defined in more or less the same intellectual and interest framework as in "genuine" market economies.

The second part of the book presents the results of interviews with the managers of typical Hungarian enterprises. These interviews were carried out in 1991, with reinterviews, whose results we also report, begun in the spring of 1992. The interviews sought to elicit information about the problems Hungarian firms were facing and the measures that were being taken to deal with them. In some firms, strategies for survival and growth were in place, although only time can tell whether these strategies will be successful. Other firms had no strategies other than a policy of "drifting," continuing operations in the old way, incurring losses and depleting assets. While the lack of responsiveness of these drifting firms is some cause for dismay, it must be borne in mind that the birth and death of firms is a natural and necessary part of the renewal of the economy.

This book is the result of research undertaken as part of a World Bank project on Enterprise Behavior and Economic Reforms in Central and Eastern Europe. The authors are grateful to their colleagues at the World Bank, at the Research Institute for Industrial Economics of the Hungarian Academy of Science, and at Arizona State University for advice and suggestions. Judit Kóczián provided capable research assistance and Richard Laborin expertly typed successive drafts of the book.

Firms Afloat and Firms Adrift

Chapter 1

Hungarian Industrial Development in the 1980s

1.1 Main Policy Issues of the 1980s

The economic policy issues of the 1980s were increasingly centered around the necessity of economic reform. For obvious political reasons, the reform could not seriously include any significant measure aimed at changing the dominance of state property in the economy. Instead, the key concept of economic policy was the creation of a market economy, or, in a more microeconomic approach, market construction. It is therefore particularly interesting to see how issues that were initially key, such as price reform, were pushed to the background while topics such as entrepreneurship, which touched much more on the sensitive problem of the structure of property rights, came increasingly to the fore. Our overview might also be instructive in showing that the reform process was understood in a strongly institutional manner, while basic macropolicy orientations and options were tackled much less by reformers.

Price Reform and Market Construction

Hungary's 1968 reform abandoning mandatory planning did not really break with the centralist tradition in the field of pricing. Three categories of prices were introduced: so-called free, maximum (or ceiling), and officially fixed prices. Consumers were probably most aware of the second and third categories. The 1968 reform could not eliminate the substantial difference that existed between producer and consumer prices, so the two-tiered price system was maintained. Ideas of a currency policy reform, including the short-term introduction of forint convertibility, were effectively dropped by the 1970s. Thus, contrary to the original reform intentions, the price system remained highly isolated from the world market. Perhaps the main reason for this was the fundamental change in international price structures that began in 1973, which put the Hungarian price system under enormous and fast-growing pressure.

The changes in the price system were basically compatible with the framework for the regulation of the firms' activities provided by the New Economic Mechanism (NEM) in 1968. Unlike enterprises in other socialist economies at that time, Hungarian enterprises enjoyed a high level of formal independence from the government and its main arm of microeconomic intervention, the State Planning Office (or National Planning Board, as it has been called in some English texts). Enterprises were formally free to prepare their own plans, which had to be discussed with their sectoral ministry and the planning agency of the government. The state organs were not allowed under NEM to give formal orders to firms. What they could do was to influence managers personally by, for example, linking their annual bonuses to the degree of conformity of enterprise-level plans and performances to governmental plans.

If such personal influence proved insufficient, another "line of command" was still available. This was the internal communications system of the Communist Party. Until the late 1980s, a great majority of managers were Party members who had vowed obedience to decisions coming from above. Therefore, a command transmitted from a ministry to the regional economic secretary of the Party and retransmitted to the manager effectively did not leave any ground for discussion. Managers had to maximize at least two things: the annual profit of the firm, which was a major factor in determining their annual bonuses; and the enterprise's compliance with the expectations of the government, which, like increasing exports to the West when more currency receipts were needed, increasing domestic sales when shortage was a threat, increasing imports from CMEA countries when the macrolevel trade balance was too positive for Hungary, etc., were often contrary to the profit-maximization requirement.

The development of NEM included several stages in which either the formal or the informal elements of the enterprises' dependence on the government were emphasized. The formal dependence of a number of enterprises increased in 1972 when 50 big industrial firms were given the special status of having a direct link of command established between them and the government. A step in the opposite direction was taken in 1980, when the three sectoral ministries of industry were amalgamated into one. This was meant to eliminate the competition for funds and influence among the branch ministries of industry and to weaken the sector-specific character of industrial-policy measures.

The system of competitive pricing introduced in 1980 was based on the assumption that domestic demand and exports to socialist countries would be successfully regulated. Thus the only scope for enterprise growth would be exports for convertible currency, and microeconomic performance in this respect would determine the extent to which enterprises could try to increase profits on the domestic and CMEA markets.

The new pricing system was built on a nominal anchor. In stabilization programs of the 1980s such as those in Argentina and in Israel, this was the exchange rate. Hungary, instead, preferred to choose the price of a product fundamental for the world economy and having an exact equivalent on the domestic market: Saudi light petrol FOB Ras Tanura.

The pricing of the majority of raw and other materials was based on convertible-currency import prices. A pivotal element of the system was the so-called export-dependent pricing principle for manufactured goods. The entire machinery industry, the clothing industry, and some important enterprises in heavy chemistry belonged to the scope of validity of this principle. The principle said that within the branches where it applies, every enterprise with convertible-currency exports equaling more than 5 percent of domestic sales had to apply a pricing formula in accordance with which prices and profitability in convertible-currency sales had to serve as a benchmark price for other sales as well.

The system softened considerably already during the year of its introduction because the authorities applied several sectoral- and enterprise-level exceptions to the clear rules of the system. In subsequent years a strange sort of firms' adjustment to this regulation, instead of the prices of the world market, became more and more widespread. Those firms that were near the 5-percent limit very often succeeded in getting below it by abandoning less profitable convertible-currency exports, thus making themselves exempt from the need to connect their domestic prices to the prices they were able to obtain on Western markets. Thus a rather general trend of turning toward softer markets was clearly observable. Other exporting firms forced barter agreements with apparently high export prices on their Western trade partners in order to be able to increase domestic prices to reflect these seemingly "profitable" hard-currency exports. But probably the key reason why the whole system gradually lost importance and was finally extinguished in 1987 was that firms with substantial exports to the West threatened the authorities with increasing the efficiency of these sales by simply dropping the lowest-priced part of them. These usually successful efforts at persuasion resulted in a situation where the functioning of the new pricing system was completely distorted by subsidies or other preferences given to important hard-currency exporters to encourage them to keep up the volume of hard-currency exports despite the need to charge low prices in the West. It turned out that the given pricing system could help to apply profitability criteria for convertible-currency exports only as a one-way street. Less profitable exports could really be eliminated, but their replacement with other exports was uncertain and could not be achieved with the given set of regulations in a way that did not rely on central *dirigisme*.

The increasingly formal and irrelevant character of the 1980 pricing system became widely evident by the mid-1980s, and it is interesting to see how authorities and enterprises tried to reform it without changing the system itself. Two such attempts can be mentioned. The so-called Price Club was established in 1984 for enterprises that belonged to the export-dependent pricing system but that were interested in more freedom in determining their domestic prices. Enterprises had to apply for membership in this rather grotesque club, which was founded to serve as a grouping of enterprises with genuinely market-conforming pricing behavior. Application for membership had to include a detailed presentation of pricing, marketing, production, and R&D practices and a serious promise not to exceed in domestic sales the prices of competitive imports. The fulfillment of this latter promise was regularly controlled by authorities, but it often proved to be an impossible task because out of several million sorts of goods produced in Hungary only several tens of thousands had a clearly identifiable counterpart or substitute on the world market. Therefore, product substitutability was frequently a matter of subjective judgment by staff members of the National Board for Prices and Materials.

The other effort to bypass the increasingly formal price system was made by a group of machinery firms in order to break the pricing cartel of domestic iron and steel producers. These firms had seen many times before, and also saw in 1986, that Hungarian iron and steel enterprises nominally followed world market prices in their domestic sales to machinery industry but occasional imports of iron and steel could normally be obtained for 10–40 percent less than these official prices due to informal price cutting among exporters resulting from a continuously depressed world market for steel products.

Some engineering enterprises realized that the Hungarian pricing system effectively served as an umbrella protecting their domestic suppliers from following informal price cuts quite usual on international markets at that time. The government and the Chamber of Commerce apparently endorsed the machinery firms' initiative, admitting that artificially high domestic iron and steel prices negatively affect the competitiveness of machinery exports. But iron and steel producers could defend their positions, and their prices, by showing that exact documentation existed only for quite high official world market prices.

This system of competitive pricing was nothing more than an episode in the Hungarian reform history of the 1980s. The official abandonment of this system in March 1987 was only a recognition of the fact that further streamlining of the pricing framework based on a simulation of the market would lead nowhere, and that it was impossible to replace an efficient market regulation system with generally valid anti-monopolistic rules of pricing and competition. The observance of these rules in a socialist economy with clear and efficient markets would then have been less of a legal obligation than a result of the economy's openness to import competition. The rapid liberalization of imports and domestic prices in 1989, 1990, and 1991, along with privatization and other significant steps of progress toward a market economy, made it clear that extensive price liberalization had no reasonable alternative in terms of any "price reform" trying to emulate liberalization.

Steps Toward Institutional Reform

The establishment in 1980 of a single Ministry of Industry from the earlier ministries of heavy industry, light industry, and the iron and steel and machinery industries, respectively, was a reform measure favorably commented upon around the world, but it did not prove to be a very far-reaching change. In fact, the structure of the new ministry preserved some important relics from the earlier system. Proof of the continuing preponderance of capital- and energy-intensive industries was the fact that the two successive ministers of industry between 1980 and 1987 were a former general secretary of the Iron- and Steelworkers' Trade Union and the former director of a huge mining enterprise who was also known as a renowned expert in geological prospecting.

The quite slow institutional reforms between 1980 and 1987 also included the degradation of the Ministry of Labor to the rank of a National Office for Labor and Wages headed by a state secretary, although this office regained its status of a ministry in 1990, as well as the separation of the Hungarian Mail from the Ministry of Communications and Transport, among other changes. These reforms did not touch the role and the institutional weight of key governmental bodies responsible for economic policy. So a system was maintained in which the National Planning Board was sort of a superministry headed by a deputy prime minister and the Ministry of Finance held the responsibility for fiscal regulation and the budget. However, the National Planning Board was less of a classical planning institution than sort of a Ministry of Economic Affairs, since directive planning was limited to such sectors of the economy as infrastructure, housing, etc., but planning in this sense rather meant a distribution of budget funds related to specific targets. The Planning Board acted as a background institution preparing materials for the sessions of a special kind of economic policy-making cabinet called the State Planning Committee.

The situation was complicated by the fact that two roughly parallel bodies existed with not always clearly distinguishable profiles. One was the Economic Committee, with a responsibility for such day-to-day operative decisions as issuing import licenses in times of serious currency shortage, determining the ranking list for extraordinary import demands, etc., as a governmental body. The other was called the Economic Policy Committee, which was created by the Party and rather oriented toward economic strategy formulation. A certain part of the responsibilities of the latter two bodies was obviously shared by the Planning Committee.

Much more important changes in the governmental structure were introduced by the government taking office in May 1990, after the first democratic elections. The government of József Antall created an economic policy-making system without any sort of economic superministry. The National Planning Board was eliminated, and its departments were transferred to the remaining sectoral ministries and to the Ministry of Finance. This latter ministry officially became the governmental agency in charge of coordinating economic policy making;

therefore it inherited the Planning Board departments dealing with macropolicy issues, regulation, and macrolevel analysis and forecasting. The finance minister also became the head of the government's "economic cabinet," a narrower body consisting of ministers holding economic portfolios.

The first six months spent in office by the new government were not exempt from tensions among several top economic advisers and decision makers within the government. The primary role of the minister of finance in economic policy making was not clear yet, and the head of the prime minister's economic advisory office seemed to be successfully competing with him for the role of the chief economic guru in the country. The dispute was finally resolved by the resignation of both these high-level economic policy officials in late 1990, and the new finance minister, Mihály Kupa, became the unquestioned number one in economic policy.

The other novelty in the command structure of the economy goes back a little to the last months of the socialist government, which created the State Property Agency and gave it its current paragovernmental status. This agency, as the supposed mastermind, coordinator, and administrator of the privatization process, reports to the prime minister, but it ultimately depends on the parliament. Therefore, it cannot interfere institutionally with ministries or other governmental agencies. This fact seems to be having a favorable impact on the transparency of the privatization process, but it is also true that conflicts of interest, first of all lower-level ones, between the agency and the different ministries are sometimes quite difficult to resolve.

The institutional structure of policy making in industry and trade also underwent significant changes. The former Ministry of Foreign Trade remained in place, but it was renamed and given a more broadly defined scope of responsibility. Its new name, Ministry of International Economic Relations, suggests it is supposed to deal with economic diplomacy, international capital transactions, the promotion of foreign direct investment, etc. Its new functions may give rise to conflicts of interest with other ministries, above all those of finance and industry.

Furthermore, the redefinition of the functions of the former Ministry of Industry did, and might again in the future, lead to even more significant tensions within the government. The reason is that the former Ministry of Domestic Trade, also in control of tourism, was incorporated into the new Ministry of Industry and Trade. Trade policy issues now nominally belong to both the Ministry of International Economic Relations and the Ministry of Industry and Trade, with their fiscal aspects controlled by the Ministry of Finance. Although export promotion evidently is part of the field of competence of the Ministry of International Economic Relations, it is far less clear which of the two trade-related ministries should tackle problems of market protection, antidumping policy, and import regulation in case of necessity. This controversial institutional and legal situation has some negative implications for industrial policy making as well, since industrial policy has been becoming more and more linked to trade policy across the world economy with the widespread emergence of strategic trade policies.

The internal transformation of the ministries' decision-making structure has also had significant impacts on the way the Ministry of Industry and Trade fulfills its tasks linked to industrial policy and the fostering of structural changes. The bottom line is that the ministry completely lost its role of command over, and its right of direct interference with, the management even of state enterprises that had not yet adopted a corporate structure (which they were obliged to do before December 31, 1992, according to the law). It can influence industry only through strategic measures affecting the state-owned part of that industry; one of the most appropriate tools for this purpose is the State Assets Management Corporation established in the summer of 1992.

The command structure of the ministry shows that it has a very low level of influence on developments in manufacturing. All Hungarian ministries now have two state secretaries, one of whom, the so-called political state secretary, has no direct influence on the internal functioning of the ministry. His job is to help and represent the ministry politically, and he himself is politically dependent on the government, being appointed as part of it and leaving office together with it. The administrative state secretary is the person of linkage between the politically determined structure of the government and the permanent staff of the ministry. The four state undersecretaries of each ministry are his direct subordinates, and they are the heads of the different lines of command within the ministry.

The division of responsibilities among the four state undersecretaries in the Ministry of Industry and Trade well exemplifies the rather vague character of industrial policy making in the current Hungarian governmental organization. Tourism and energy, as fields where governmental influence supposedly can be more direct, are covered by one undersecretary each. Manufacturing, on the other hand, is split, with one undersecretary in charge of strategic and international issues and the other supervising regulatory matters. A more probing analysis of the workings of the ministry would show that one of its primary concerns is to avoid any suspicion that it might claim a role of direct control over manufacturing. This is perhaps the main reason why it has not yet managed to present a clear-cut concept of industrial policy; what has been elaborated is a document formulating industrial-policy objectives and tools only in very general terms.

Policies Influencing Entrepreneurship

A bill adopted in 1982 gave rise to quite novel types of small enterprises, mostly based on cooperative-type ownership forms. These, called GMs and VGMs (literally translated as "working communities" and "intra-enterprise working communities," respectively), were a product of a rather ambiguous governmental attitude. That government, and practically all the subsequent ones, insisted on central control of microlevel wage and purchasing-power growth on the one hand but wished to stimulate nonstate—that is, private and, to a lesser extent, cooperative—entrepreneurial dynamism on the other.

The GMs are a kind of small cooperative enterprise with the possibility and the right to transform themselves into normal cooperatives. VGMs proved to be a rather original device. Generally, their members worked extra hours for the state enterprise employing them, but this time not as its employees but as members of a subcontracting enterprise—the VGM. The tricky thing was that they were paid two to four times more per hour than what they received in their normal working time because they were not subject to the official wage-regulation system as legal members of a nonstate firm. The spread of VGMs across the national economy did eliminate some important shortage and capacity-utilization problems. They did not, however, fulfill expectations that they would upset traditional intra-enterprise political relationships and the rigid enterprise structure. Moreover, when the introduction of the new tax system in 1988–89 made VGMs subject to corporate taxation, most of them closed down.

The introduction of GMs and VGMs led to a temporary flourishing of small enterprises; their number grew from hardly more than 2,000 to more than 35,000 between 1982 and 1986. Their appearance in

Hungarian industry contributed to a partial elimination of supply bottlenecks, but the government's attitude toward them remained quite unclear. Their fiscal burdens were increased several times under the slogan of creating equal competitive conditions for all sorts of enterprises, and the problem of their identity was far from being solved even in 1988. They seem to have been another result of the pre-1990 governments' striving to replace market forces with liberal attitudes where it proved most necessary. These uncoordinated reform steps made real, profound, general reforms more difficult since they increased the number of firms, transactions, and groups of workers who were subject to special rules or who were treated as special cases.

A government policy change of a more strategic character was the elimination of many monopolistic enterprise conglomerates, or trusts; between 1980 and 1985 their number decreased from 24 to 9, with more than 4,000 new enterprises emerging either as their successors or as newly independent units of state enterprises (Wass von Czege 1987, p. 133), and many more arose through the introduction of formal self-management in a great number of state enterprises.

The 1985 Act on Enterprise Management Boards may be understood as a sort of compromise between reform economists who wanted state enterprises to have legal independence from ministries and the government's wish to maintain a measure of control over enterprise behavior. In the new system, state-owned enterprises, except for some of strategic importance, were invited to elect to their boards of management their own managers and managers of other state-owned enterprises, and enterprise directors legally became employees of these boards. Their supervisory ministry was authorized to refuse to accept the newly elected director, in which case further elections with new candidates were to be held, although this almost never happened. The strategy of the enterprise had to be worked out by the board, and its tactical realization became a task of the director.

This new scheme, however, did not change the informal dependence of enterprises on central authorities. This informal dependence was assured, as described earlier, by the personal subordination of managers to government agencies instead of by the institutional subordination of their firms to the same agencies. Moreover, optimistic expectations of better management resulting from a certain degree of independence between directors and boards of management proved unrealistic in many enterprises. In such firms, directors and boards formed Yugoslav-type redistributive coalitions, realizing that salary increases of members of the management board depended on the director's decisions while the bonuses of the director were decided upon by the board. The formation of these coalitions proved once again that radical reformers were right to assume that any change in the management system of state enterprises would be inefficient or even counterproductive if it did not create a strong interest in every employee to increase the value of the enterprise's assets. This idea of the creation of asset interest within enterprises (cf., Antal 1985) was discussed and supported by many reform economists and meant a revision of the key principle of the 1968 reform. This principle was to substitute the profit target for the plan-fulfillment target of state enterprises, but it failed to specify for what purposes increased profits would be used. It was ultimately the problem of the use of profits that made it clear that the efficient use of resources, and, among them, capital generated from profits, could not be entirely guaranteed under state ownership.

State firms where the owner was represented only by managers interested in maximizing their personal incomes proved, in most cases, unable to operate in a way that was favorable to the owner, because the increase of assets was usually thought to be only the state's task. This task could presumably be fulfilled through investment paid for, or subsidized by, the state, whereas the firm's current income seemed to be considered by the managers first of all as a source of financing current operating costs. This means that it was in their interest to increase costs, eventually to a break-even level, in order to make profits seemingly disappear, because this helped them obtain financial support from the state for investment, and thus they did not need to invest from profits.

It is curious to note that before 1989 enterprise creation in Hungary was, at least theoretically, still governed by the 1875 Corporation Act. Some of its clauses were completely outdated and some others had been repealed after 1945 for political reasons. So any change in the form of functioning of Hungarian enterprises, as, for instance, the Bankruptcy Act of 1987, could only add to the legal confusion in this matter until the adoption of the new Corporation Act. This bill, specifying the legal status and exact property form of enterprises, was adopted in the autumn of 1988. The Corporation Act, or Law on Economic Associations, defined legal corporate forms such as joint-stock company, company limited by shares, limited-liability company, etc., and it provided legal guarantees in conformity with international standards for the protection and safety of private assets in firms.

The legislation on privatization gained speed thereafter. The creation of the legal framework for privatization as well as for the launching of new ventures has been of utmost importance for changes in the behavioral attitudes of different forms of corporate management in Hungary. It facilitated, for example, the widespread transition from clerk-type to entrepreneur-type behavioral patterns among managers, even in nominally state-owned firms. This observation is based on evidence from companies such as the Transdanubian Oil and Gas Equipment Factory, Salgglas, DUNAFERR, RABA, Gedeon Richter, and others, but it has a strong legal background in the formerly unknown direct and complete financial liability of managers, if they are board members, for the consequences of their decisions.

"Nominally state-owned firms" is a term applied to former state enterprises whose legal status was determined by the 1977 Act on State Enterprises with its Amendment in 1985 that have already adopted a corporate form. All Hungarian firms were obliged to transform themselves into corporations—that is, to undergo the so-called transformation process, in conformity with the Law on Transformation of 1989—before the end of 1992. The influence of the state on their management is much less direct and formal than in the case of state enterprises, because legally prescribed decision-making processes have to be observed in each of them, even if the state has a 100-percent ownership stake in such a firm. In joint-stock companies, for example, major strategic decisions can be taken only by the General Assembly. Convocation of the General Assembly has to be announced six weeks in advance; this fact alone enormously reduces the speed and ease with which the state can intervene in the functioning of the management.

The existence of 100-percent state-owned corporate entities makes it necessary to view the privatization process as a two-tiered structure. Transformation of a state-owned enterprise into a corporation is a prerequisite for privatization, and sometimes the two acts take place simultaneously; but transformation itself does not necessarily create a private firm. Privatization itself should be understood as a not absolutely necessary consequence of enterprise transformation, which results in a less than 100-percent ownership stake of the state in the new firm.

This quite flexible concept of privatization, or private ownership, has to be used in examining behavioral patterns of Hungarian enterprises, because, at least according to our knowledge of Hungarian industry, even a nominal injection of private capital into a 100-percent state-owned firm makes it even more open for further privatization. It changes the attitude of the management, which becomes governed by its interest in attracting more private capital. This is why we can consider as privatization those injections of capital where the investor is either another Hungarian firm with a state majority ownership or a foreign investor operating as a public firm. This is not a rarity in Hungary, where Austrian Industries and ENI of Italy, both state-owned industrial holdings, have been active as investors.

The legal framework of privatization includes two more legal pieces defining the role of foreign investors and the Hungarian state in the process. The Law on Entrepreneurship with Foreign Participation, adopted in 1988 and amended in 1990, makes possible even 100-percent foreign ownership in Hungarian firms, and it clears the road for the, if need be, complete repatriation of profits and guarantees important tax allowances for joint ventures (JVs).

The Law on Entrepreneurship with Foreign Participation created the conditions for firms with partial or full foreign stock ownership to become legal entities in compliance with the Law on Economic Associations. The major changes brought about by this law have been the following:

—no permission is required for creating a JV with minority foreign ownership; the authorization procedure for JVs with majority foreign ownership is much simpler than in the previous system;

—the foreign partner can have an equity share of up to 100 percent;

—the foreign investor is not obliged to create a new firm; instead, an already existing firm can be transformed into a JV;

—the foreign partner is entitled to import investment goods without an import license up to the amount of the cash he committed to the equity capital of the JV, although this preference for JVs lost most of its importance when import liberalization became practically an across-the-board system from January 1, 1991;

—Hungarian nationals, i.e., not only legal entities, can become co-owners of JVs;

—foreign nationals are allowed to buy shares of Hungarian firms even if these are traded only in Hungary.

The role of the Hungarian state in privatization was defined in the laws of July 1990 and August 1990, on the Creation of the State

Property Agency (SPA) and the Protection of State Property, respectively. These laws gave the SPA the right to control, in principle, the entire privatization process of productive assets, but the SPA can exercise this right only for transactions above a HUF 5 million value, except for sales of land and real estate. Enterprise transformation without privatization then means that the SPA takes the shares of newly established joint-stock companies into its portfolio. Subsequent privatization means the sale of these assets by the SPA.

1.2 Some Major Trends in Industrial Activity

Trends in industrial sales and output in the 1980s show only modest growth in the first half of the decade. Table 1 reports export sales of Hungarian industry in total and by sector for the 1980s. In nominal terms, all the sectors except for the miscellaneous (category) exhibited some growth. As Table 2 shows, total sales followed a pattern similar to that of exports. However, as Table 3 shows, prices of industry's output also grew considerably during the 1980s, particularly at the beginning and end of the decade. The products of electrical engineering, mining, and metallurgy sectors experienced the largest price increases, while those of the miscellaneous, chemical, and engineering sectors increased the least. When, as in Table 4, Hungarian industry is considered in terms of real output, the problem facing this industry becomes more evident. Over the decade of the 1980s, total industrial output increased by 10.8 percent in real terms. Mining and miscellaneous industry suffered absolute declines, and by 1989 real output in all sectors of industry was declining.

An unpublished analysis of firms oriented toward the CMEA market carried out at the Institute of World Economy of the Hungarian Academy of Sciences hinted as early as in 1983 at the danger of a collapse of traditional sales to Eastern Europe. Case studies prepared a few years later (cf., Inotai 1985; Pártos 1985; Rácz 1985; Török 1985; Meisel and Mohácsi 1990) gave interesting insights into how managers were aware of the danger but also into the extent to which most of them were unable to prevent the crisis.

The profound crisis in Hungarian industry that began in 1988–89 was not, for most firms, a sudden awakening from a pleasant dream of steady growth but a more or less logical consequence of time and money wasted in the 1980s. It is true that reform steps were only

Table 1

Hungarian Export Sales, 1980-89 (current prices, million Ft.)

	1980	1981	1982	1983	1984	1985
Mining Industry	3587	3349	3280	3209	3083	3130
Electrical Engineering Ind.	215	328	88	98	98	150
Metallurgy Industry	19990	17255	17696	20108	25971	24307
Engineering Industry	85471	89954	100422	110551	122719	138122
Building Material Industry	2678	2747	2720	3026	3292	3087
Chemical Industry	32830	35089	37642	48725	59280	64311
Light Industry	29106	29311	29951	32552	36264	38423
Miscellaneous Industry	1209	1448	917	817	857	960
Food Processing Industry	30967	34446	38681	41981	47522	42362
INDUSTRY TOTAL	206053	213927	231397	261067	299086	314852

Table 1 (cont.)

		of which			of which			of which	
	1986	rubles	non-rubles	1987	rubles	non-rubles	1988	rubles	non-rubles
Mining Industry	3281	1988	1293	3441	1992	1449	3594	1943	1651
Electrical Engineering Ind.	179	148	31	156	143	13	172	162	10
Metallurgy Industry	24811	6897	17914	26213	6616	19597	40831	7881	32950
Engineering Industry	145646	109886	35760	149325	108053	41272	156348	106883	49465
Building Material Industry	3528	876	2652	4070	635	3435	5341	578	4763
Chemical Industry	56684	21890	34794	64534	21047	43437	77218	20865	56353
Light Industry	40764	18674	22090	46030	17628	28402	49257	16430	32827
Miscellaneous Industry	1015	508	507	1004	472	532	860	232	628
Food Processing Industry	40536	16189	24347	44415	15058	29357	52195	17526	34669
INDUSTRY TOTAL	316444	177056	139388	339188	171644	167544	385816	172500	213316

Table 2

Sales of Hungarian Industry, by Sector (at current prices, million Ft.)

	1980	1981	1982	1983	1984	1985	1986	1987	1988	1989
Mining Industry	56137	65027	75213	78758	81523	91737	90486	93794	94060	86138
Electrical Engineering Ind.	39484	45594	52400	59713	62703	71865	66574	77329	101141	100749
Metallurgy Industry	90154	84801	88238	91435	99520	103760	108254	115535	155370	167667
Engineering Industry	209034	223790	243187	255819	274406	307222	335673	363001	366807	399382
Building Material Industry	29527	31561	32440	33365	37528	37380	39739	43902	53050	50188
Chemical Industry	173667	198750	215420	232137	251504	266035	248514	263675	331762	312236
Light Industry	129053	136682	135622	141066	151995	165417	171214	185327	201445	204914
Miscellaneous Industry	12419	13799	13712	11558	12195	12394	12432	12949	8136	11545
Food Processing Industry	171222	179518	191135	200400	217802	221537	226604	246892	311886	292356
INDUSTRY TOTAL	910697	979522	1047367	1104251	1189176	1277347	1299490	1402404	1623657	1625176

Table 3

Price Indices of Hungarian Industrial Sales (previous year = 100)

	1980	1981	1982	1983	1984	1985	1986	1987	1988	1989	1990
Mining Industry	164.1	121.8	113.5	107.6	104.0	105.1	100.9	102.1	102.7	107.0	130.8
Electrical Engineering Ind.	129.7	112.8	113.4	109.0	100.7	112.6	111.2	114.0	114.9	103.7	126.8
Metallurgy Industry	125.3	101.4	104.2	104.7	105.7	104.7	102.0	104.3	110.4	127.4	118.4
Engineering Industry	100.1	102.7	102.2	105.2	105.0	105.3	105.0	104.1	99.1	113.5	112.1
Building Material Industry	110.3	108.3	103.7	105.8	105.9	104.1	105.6	102.8	100.8	112.3	122.6
Chemical Industry	135.8	112.1	107.0	105.8	102.9	102.7	94.1	98.8	106.8	113.9	123.5
Light Industry	100.6	102.2	101.7	103.0	105.5	106.3	103.9	104.7	104.1	114.3	118.2
Miscellaneous Industry	101.8	103.6	103.0	101.0	102.1	103.6	102.4	107.3	100.9	115.7	109.3
Food Processing Industry	111.4	104.2	101.4	104.8	103.4	101.3	103.2	104.9	105.1	117.9	188.4
INDUSTRY TOTAL	115.0	106.5	104.6	105.3	104.1	104.4	102.0	103.7	104.5	114.6	120.9

Table 4

Sales of Hungarian Industry, by Sector (in constant 1980 prices, million Ft.)

	1980	1981	1982	1983	1984	1985	1986	1987	1988	1989
Mining Industry	56137	53388	54502	52855	52595	56280	55174	56164	54868	46814
Electrical Engineering Ind.	39484	40972	40938	42958	44788	45484	37826	38665	43974	42154
Metallurgy Industry	90154	83630	83243	82374	85060	85049	86603	88873	107896	91621
Engineering Industry	209034	217907	231607	232563	236557	251821	262245	272933	277884	266255
Building Material Industry	29527	27264	28964	28038	29748	28534	28796	30917	37098	31173
Chemical Industry	173667	156161	179517	182785	191682	198534	197233	210940	249445	205418
Light Industry	129053	128283	130444	131837	134509	137848	136971	141471	148121	132202
Miscellaneous Industry	12419	12199	12815	10702	11086	10872	10626	10359	6457	7962
Food Processing Industry	171222	153700	180316	180541	191054	190980	188837	195946	236277	187408
INDUSTRY TOTAL	910697	919738	943574	943804	974734	1005785	999608	1038818	1151530	1009426

hesitantly taken by the government, and most of them took place only after 1986. There were, however, very few enterprises that were able to use their limited freedom of action to prepare their own adjustment to the world market before *de facto* entering it. As it turned out, these successful firms—for example, Tungsram, Lehel, Styl, and Chinoin—were mostly picked up by foreign investors in the first phase of the Hungarian privatization process. It therefore would not be an exaggeration to say that their microlevel adjustment prepared these companies for privatization.

The low growth of industrial output would not have been a problem *per se*, but it was distributed quite evenly across Hungarian industry. This is why there was not much structural change in this sector during the 1980s, either in the macro or the micro sense. The branch structure of gross output (see Table 5) did not undergo significant changes in the course of the decade. It is quite remarkable that a few energy- and capital-intensive sectors, such as mining and metallurgy, managed to regain their share of 1980 nominal gross output in 1988 or 1989 after a temporary fall during the decade.

Favorable structural trends, such as the growing share of engineering in industrial output, were also reversed by 1988–89. The only technology-intensive branch of industry emerging as a clear winner from macro-structural changes in the 1980s was electrical engineering, but its apparently good performance deserves two points of explanation:

(a) Its spectacular development was mainly CMEA-market oriented, and it could be called technology intensive only in a special sense, i.e., according to the quite low quality and performance standards of CMEA markets.

(b) This industry was far from being able to join the club of "flag-ship" sectors of Hungarian industry, such as nonelectrical engineering, the chemical industry, light industry, or the food sector. Its structural weight was still of minor importance, and the not entirely organic character of its dynamic development in the 1980s has been demonstrated by the exceptionally serious crisis that overtook it after 1989.

The investment trends of the 1980s give the impression that Hungarian industry was increasingly seriously undercapitalized. Investment growth, even in nominal terms, as reported in Table 6, was low, and, in real terms, Table 7 reveals that a number of sectors suffered sharp declines in capital formation. For most branches, real gross investment reached its lowest level in the decade in 1988; the volume

Table 5

Share Structure of Hungarian Industry's Sales (%)

	1980	1981	1982	1983	1984	1985	1986	1987	1988	1989
Mining Industry	6.1	6.6	7.2	7.1	6.8	7.2	7.0	6.7	5.8	5.3
Electrical Engineering Ind.	4.3	4.7	5.0	5.4	5.3	5.6	5.1	5.5	6.2	6.2
Metallurgy Industry	9.9	8.7	8.4	8.3	8.4	8.1	8.3	8.3	9.6	10.3
Engineering Industry	23.0	22.8	23.2	23.2	23.1	24.1	25.8	25.9	22.6	24.6
Building Material Industry	3.2	3.2	3.1	3.0	3.2	2.9	3.1	3.1	3.3	3.1
Chemical Industry	19.1	20.3	20.6	21.0	21.1	20.8	19.1	18.8	20.4	19.2
Light Industry	14.2	14.0	13.0	12.8	12.8	13.0	13.2	13.2	12.4	12.6
Miscellaneous Industry	1.4	1.4	1.3	1.1	1.0	1.0	1.0	0.9	0.5	0.7
Food Processing Industry	18.8	18.3	18.2	18.1	18.3	17.3	17.4	17.6	19.2	18.0
INDUSTRY TOTAL	100.0	100.0	100.0	100.0	100.0	100.0	100.0	100.0	100.0	100.0

Table 6

Investment in Hungarian Industry (current prices, million Ft.)

	1980	1981	1982	1983	1984	1985	1986	1987	1988	1989
Mining Industry	9899	9456	9892	11995	14067	16940	16610	16890	16345	15696
Electrical Engineering Ind.	13914	12856	13511	15542	15668	15682	13690	15881	11628	14360
Metallurgy Industry	8567	7327	5544	5958	5866	4367	4101	3505	3895	6662
Engineering Industry	12046	10594	11164	11373	11026	9430	9721	13910	10557	11661
Building Material Industry	3406	2518	2320	2670	2547	3184	2398	2541	3264	6697
Chemical Industry	7922	8854	11047	11067	10722	13488	13450	15842	16383	18050
Light Industry	5016	5381	7091	5532	5302	4727	6076	5803	5581	8398
Miscellaneous Industry	807	1010	812	609	439	381	315	426	591	1019
Food Processing Industry	8679	8193	7741	7130	7952	8656	9278	9598	12261	16019
INDUSTRY TOTAL	70256	66189	69122	71876	73589	76855	75639	84396	80505	98362

Table 7

Index of Real Investment in Hungarian Industry (1980 = 100)

	1980	1981	1982	1983	1984	1985	1986	1987	1988	1989
Mining Industry	100	93.3	92.9	105.9	118.6	136.0	126.2	122.5	115.5	97.1
Electrical Engineering Ind.	100	91.0	91.8	98.4	95.5	92.1	78.6	87.5	62.9	69.0
Metallurgy Industry	100	84.5	61.3	61.7	58.3	41.6	37.5	30.2	32.5	48.5
Engineering Industry	100	85.8	86.1	83.1	76.8	62.7	60.3	80.4	60.2	58.8
Building Material Industry	100	72.1	63.8	69.0	62.9	74.5	53.3	52.9	65.3	122.4
Chemical Industry	100	109.5	130.4	122.2	112.4	136.2	128.5	141.0	142.3	140.0
Light Industry	100	100.0	133.1	96.9	88.9	75.6	91.7	82.6	75.1	100.6
Miscellaneous Industry	100	121.3	92.2	65.8	44.8	36.9	28.8	37.2	50.6	74.7
Food Processing Industry	100	92.0	83.8	73.0	76.9	78.9	80.1	77.9	96.0	107.3
INDUSTRY TOTAL	100	91.9	92.2	90.0	88.0	87.8	82.1	86.5	80.4	86.8

of gross real overall industrial investment was then almost 20 percent below its 1980 level. Surprisingly enough, mining did not belong to the losers; along with the also highly capital-intensive chemical industry, it got increasing bits of a shrinking pie (see Table 8).

The iron and steel industry was ostensibly badly neglected by investment policy. Deeper analysis would be needed to see whether, if iron and steel had retained its average share of total industrial investment over the decade, such investments would have been sufficient to stop the dramatic degradation of its capacities. If, however, its rapidly falling share in industrial investment is compared with its almost constant percentage within industrial output, it becomes quite evident that a rapidly aging capital stock was more and more intensively exploited to achieve levels of output that did not decrease, even in relative terms.

Separate figures for ruble and nonruble exports are available in a sectoral breakdown only from 1986 onward. They can be seen in Table 1, which shows that the shrinking of exports to the CMEA region had started long before this trading system was finally dissolved. The process started in 1986–87 with the first decrease of the ratio of ruble exports to nonruble exports in decades for most branches, but it accelerated only in the terminal stages of the agony of the CMEA system, i.e., in 1989.

A methodological remark cannot be avoided here. It might seem strange that separate figures for the ruble and nonruble exports of industrial branches are given only from 1986 on. The explanation for this is that we have used industrial statistics, which differ in concept from what are known as trade statistics. Industrial statistics do not concentrate on products but on the part of the output of a sector or subsector that is sold abroad. The Hungarian system of industrial statistics is based on each enterprise's belonging to a given sector, listed in the industrial-statistics register. For example, steel plates exported by an engineering firm are reported as engineering exports. The same export item is considered to be iron and steel exports in trade statistics.

Even such a brief analysis of the main trends of Hungarian industrial development clearly supports the conclusion that there was no sudden crisis in Hungarian industry in the late 1980s and that the slowness or even a certain reversal of structural changes together with slow output growth during the decade prepared the ground for the dramatic crisis that followed in the early 1990s. The policy framework of industrial development during the "lost decade" of the 1980s also

Table 8

Branch Structure of Industrial Investment (%)

	1980	1981	1982	1983	1984	1985	1986	1987	1988	1989
Mining Industry	14.1	14.3	14.3	16.7	19.1	22.0	22.1	20.1	20.3	15.8
Electrical Engineering Ind.	19.8	19.4	19.5	21.6	21.3	20.6	18.1	18.9	14.5	14.6
Metallurgy Industry	12.2	11.1	8.0	8.3	8.0	5.7	5.4	4.2	4.8	6.8
Engineering Industry	17.1	16.0	16.1	15.8	15.0	12.3	12.8	16.4	13.1	11.9
Building Material Industry	4.8	3.8	3.4	3.7	3.4	4.1	3.2	3.0	4.1	6.8
Chemical Industry	11.3	13.4	16.0	15.4	14.6	17.5	17.6	18.6	20.4	18.3
Light Industry	7.1	8.1	10.3	7.7	7.2	6.1	8.1	6.9	6.9	8.5
Miscellaneous Industry	1.2	1.5	1.2	0.9	0.6	0.5	0.4	0.5	0.7	1.0
Food Processing Industry	12.4	12.4	11.2	9.9	10.8	11.2	12.3	11.4	15.2	16.3
INDUSTRY TOTAL	100	100	100	100	100	100	100	100	100	100

shows that the multitude of reform steps was unable to offset the lack of a target-oriented, effective, and tough industrial policy. As a matter of fact, none of the array of different reform concepts included any significant industrial policy package.

1.3 Capital Markets, Monetary Policy, and Industry in the 1980s

Before 1981, monetary policy in Hungary was characterized by a rather liberal attitude toward overall liquidity growth. The growth of M1, M2, and the stock of credit was usually faster than that of nominal GDP (Huszti 1987, p. 105), and savings showed an even faster rate of growth. Until 1982, inflation was controlled by increasing the exchange rate of the forint *vis-à-vis* convertible currencies. This revaluation of the Hungarian currency was also a result of the country's joining the IMF and the World Bank in 1982, a precondition for which had been the creation of a unified exchange rate.

The only tools of macroeconomic demand management were rediscounting, credit rationing, and interest-rate policy carried out by the National Bank in the one-tiered banking system. Domestic monetary policy had to carry a burden more and more inappropriate to the tasks of the monetary system linked to the opening of the economy to international financial markets. In the 1970s, the administrative character of monetary policy increased due to the need to reestablish balance-of-payments equilibrium. Subsequent developments showed that "measures taken in order to enlarge and diversify international monetary relations cannot be built on a rigid domestic monetary system constrained and compressed in an administrative way" (Huszti 1987, p. 82). Official acceptance of this fact gradually led to a partial liberalization in the monetary sphere and particularly of the capital markets.

The economic mechanism introduced in 1968 made the allocation of capital mainly a task of the sectoral ministries and the central planning apparatus. Enterprises were also entitled to carry out investment projects with their own financial means, albeit under more or less strong indirect central control exerted through the National Bank. The inefficiency of capital allocation in this system was increased by the considerable financial weakness of the majority of enterprises.

Ideas for the reform of the system of capital allocation developed in four directions:

(1) a comprehensive reform of property forms and capital management by the state, based on the creation of holdings of ownership rights by quasi-public organizations;

(2) the creation of a two-tiered banking system with independent commercial banks free to collect deposits and offer credits on a capital market subject to a low level of governmental regulation;

(3) the creation of a two-tiered banking system with a strong link to the National Bank and operating on a highly regulated capital market subject to gradual liberalization; and

(4) the retention of a one-tiered banking system and a centralized credit-allocation system along with a quick liberalization of credit allocation to the enterprise sphere.

The solution finally chosen by the government was a combination of proposals (2) and (3), with a considerable emphasis on (3). It was preceded, however, by other financial liberalization measures of a rather limited scope. The creation of bank-like innovation funds, the so-called small banks, became possible in 1982, and a bond market open to enterprises and partly to the population was created in the following year.

The most far-reaching change in the financial system certainly was the establishment of legally independent commercial banks as successors to the National Bank's several specialized credit departments on January 1, 1987. This reform step was essentially based on a realization by the government of the fact that

> the [Hungarian] system of financial institutions is unable to cope with a series of important problems. These are, among other things, the creation of enterprises in general, the financing of small enterprises, the realization of innovations, the financing of leasing and of projects necessary for increasing exports, or even simple discounting. It can be increasingly felt that monetary policy operating on a global scale, which in practice is unable to handle projects already decided upon or started and loss-making production, has a set of tools inappropriate to resolve the above-mentioned problems. New tools and institutions would also be needed. (Antal and Surányi 1987, p. 7)

This analysis still holds in spite of the fact that new banks have been mushrooming and several credit facilities, Start, Egzisztencia, etc., facilitating the creation of new businesses have been established, most of them with foreign financial support. Therefore quite a few new tools and institutions are now in place, but their level of use is still very low. Several reasons can be given:

(1) The interest-rate level is generally high, up to 40 percent in early 1992, to which inappropriately high bank margins and banking costs are added.

(2) The problem of creditor protection is unresolved. Collateral equivalent to 100–150 percent of the amount of credit is requested from the would-be debtors, who mostly are private entrepreneurs with no significant savings. A partial solution to this problem might be the Credit Guarantee Fund set up by the government in the fall of 1992, but its expected volume limit of HUF 4 billion would cover only part of the needs. Moreover, an appropriate system for the evaluation of the creditworthiness of small entrepreneurs is still lacking. The simple introduction of such systems as are already operational in the West would not be helpful, because they must first be adapted to the very rapidly changing Hungarian entrepreneurial setting.

(3) A third problem is that the investment environment in the Hungarian economy as such is far from favorable. This is due to the recession and the very tough monetary restrictions as well as to outdated rules of accounting and capital accumulation. Very low rates of amortization and the legal uncertainty linked to real-estate investment, because of the legal vacuum yet to be filled by the Law on Land and Real Estate, are just two illustrations of this problem.

Five commercial banks with a general lending profile were created in the form of joint-stock companies with 100 percent of the shares owned by the state, but they will have to be partially privatized before 1995 according to the Banking Law of 1992. The first result of the appearance of new commercial banks on the Hungarian financial scene was undoubtedly inflationary. The amount of credits given to enterprises soared in early 1987 due to the efforts of the new banks to put their hands on a part of the financial market developing under restructuring (JA 1988, p. 24).

How the new commercial banks have functioned is crucial for understanding the macroeconomic conditions in which any stabilization or industrial-policy program is supposed to operate. The extent to which real entrepreneurial competition among commercial banks could unfold was already limited at the very moment of their creation by several factors (Bokros 1987, pp. 25–28). These factors are still valid, although their scope of validity is more limited due to the appearance of new banks on the Hungarian capital market as well as to the unfolding of a variety of modern capital-market institutions such as the stock exchange, an over-the-counter market, mutual funds, etc. These limitations are:

(1) huge differences in capital stock—if that of banks 1 and 2 was approximately 100 each, then bank 3 was around 35 and banks 4 as well as 5, only 15 to 17;

(2) important regional and size inequalities in national networks of branches and offices;

(3) rules of monetary creation and refinancing are the same for all five banks despite the differences in size and scope of operation.

The dependence of the commercial banks, partly on the National Bank due to the strict rules of refinancing and partly on the State Property Agency in its role as the holder of the majority of the big banks' shares, also points to an obvious lack of autonomy of the banking system in influencing monetary policy. Moreover, monetary policy has been largely unsuccessful in replacing *dirigiste* industrial policies in identifying necessary flows of investment consistent with the structural policy targets set by successive governments. Monetary policy proved unable to distinguish between sectors, subsectors, or firms with excess liquidity and those with a lack of liquidity, leading to bankruptcies in cases where both capacities and solvent demand for products were available.

One reason why monetary policy has been unable to distinguish between sectors in different situations of liquidity is that net foreign borrowing has become practically organic in the economy. This not very obvious trend created the impression that lack of liquidity had become chronic, first of all in the field of investment, and that it could be overcome only by means of loans from abroad if the anti-inflationary stance of economic policy was to be maintained (Huszti 1987, p. 179). What really happened was just the opposite. The relatively generous credit policies in the 1970s, partly linked to ambitious investment projects in the energy sector, the petrochemical industry, agriculture, etc., created excessive liquid demand for which no supply counterpart existed either in volume or in structural terms. This created a constant demand for large imports for convertible currency, and when restriction measures came in cycles or in waves (cf., Bauer 1981, 1987), the government proved unable to take back the earlier surplus liquidity already spent on imports. What it could do was restrict current liquidity. This quite often made life for enterprises more difficult and increased their financial dependence on the central bank or on the budget. Such a policy of abrupt credit restriction could only create an increase in the stock of unfinished investment into which a considerable amount of convertible-currency imports had been frozen.

The central bank's management of solvent demand was unable to direct liquidity only into those sectors with an urgent need for it and to drain it away from those where it was in excess. It became obvious that only a few enterprises were creditors and debtors to the banking system at the same time. This fact has been closely linked to another, namely, that losses of enterprises ultimately covered by a growing budget deficit, especially between 1985 and 1989, i.e., before the extensive subsidy-cutting programs of the government, did not have their counterpart in increased savings because treasury bills for financing the budget deficit from savings did not exist at that time.

Although the above-described situation remains basically valid for the monetary environment of Hungarian industry in 1992, a few complementary remarks seem appropriate to bring the picture up to date. The budget deficit could be kept more or less under governmental control in 1989, 1990, and 1991, with deficits below 3 percent of GDP each year, but there is danger of a deficit explosion in 1992. The budget deficit might eventually reach 7–8 percent of GDP by the end of the year. The reasons for this are twofold: first, the budget proposal for 1992 did not take into account appropriately the continuing recession and the impact of the new, severe bankruptcy legislation, both of which resulted in a much larger erosion of the corporate tax base than expected; and, second, tax discipline is lax, arrears in other payments to the budget are also enormous, for example, arrears in customs-duty payments amount to 2 percent of annual GDP, and the social-security budget is also in danger.

The serious budget disequilibrium seems to be threatening the financial system with considerable crowding-out effects. The interesting thing is that it does not matter for most enterprises in need of liquidity whether the budget deficit is caused by subsidies to other, nonperforming firms or by their nonpayment of taxes and customs duties. Cash-strapped firms suffer from the fact that the liquidity they expect from the banking system is kidnapped, so to speak, by the budget in the form of treasury bills, government bonds, etc. As a matter of fact, budget deficits arising from *de facto* subsidies to ailing enterprises or from their unauthorized tax debt have the same impact on other firms, and therefore they are basically seeing the same situation as existed 3–5 years ago. They are confronted by a banking system and a capital market both apparently unable to provide them with the necessary amount of liquidity.

This drought in financing exacerbates the already existing queuing problem, wherein firms delay payments to each other for lack of liquidity, because most firms faced with liquidity problems tend to become involuntary debtors to other firms. Moreover, there seems to be a vicious circle here, the existence of which might not have been completely realized by the government. The new bankruptcy legislation in effect from January 1, 1992, allows 90 days for firms to settle their debts. If they are unable to meet this deadline, they are legally bound to declare bankruptcy. This drastic piece of legal regulation of enterprise finances was enacted in order to eliminate the queuing problem, but it hits most seriously those firms whose liquidity problems are due only to their being involuntary interenterprise creditors themselves. The liquidation of such firms further erodes the tax base. This erosion indirectly increases the budget deficit with its crowding-out effects. Therefore, even more liquidity is channeled from the banking system to the budget, and queuing among enterprises may increase again.

1.4 The Regulation of Foreign Trade

The gradual liberalization of Hungarian foreign trade began in the early 1980s in keeping with the country's joining the IMF and the World Bank. The formal beginning of the liberalization process was temporarily hampered by the dramatic crisis in the foreign-currency liquidity of Hungary, which led to GATT-conforming import restrictions between September 1982 and June 1984. But the liberalization gained speed later in the 1980s. Liberalization measures included a gradual increase in the number of enterprises authorized to conclude direct trade deals in convertible currencies. As of January 1, 1988, practically every enterprise could be granted these so-called rights to foreign trade. The abolition of restrictions on the range of goods in which trading enterprises could do business, the creation of trading houses, and several steps toward a quite high degree of liberalization of joint-venture regulations so that from 1986 joint ventures could be established with a more than 50-percent foreign participation were other important steps. But case-by-case import licensing was never completely lifted prior to 1990, and it was exceptionally strong between September 1982 and June 1984 on the basis of a waiver obtained from GATT because of balance-of-payments and liquidity difficulties. A subsidy-based export-promotion policy existed instead of export-oriented industrial and trade policies.

Increases in exports were mostly the result of efforts to squeeze more and more from the given and rather obsolete production and trade structure without an appropriate exchange-rate policy and in the absence of an innovation– and capital-market–developing policy (cf., Balassa 1986, chap. 3) and with an overall decrease in export profitability. Every enterprise with relatively important convertible-currency exports was in a good bargaining position with the government. Promises to increase exports served as grounds for obtaining more subsidies and preferences such as the possibility of increasing wages or bonuses not subject to normal punitive taxes linked to wage increases exceeding centrally determined rates or simply licenses for more imports. Therefore, government efforts to increase convertible-currency exports had quite serious consequences for the state budget, especially in 1985 and 1986.

Another important field where no progress in liberalization was achieved was in trade with CMEA countries. In this trade, an export push, mainly in so-called hard goods, was traditionally very strong on the Hungarian side, and it usually exceeded the volume and value of what could really be imported. Pricing rules in this trade also made export subsidies necessary, above all in machinery and agricultural exports. Therefore, receiving a contingent right or an export license in transferable-ruble trade almost automatically meant more subsidies. Enterprise concentration in this trade was high, with mostly bigger enterprises with a considerable political weight interested in it, so withdrawing subsidies or not granting export licenses sometimes became a politically delicate matter for the government.

All attempts to try to introduce a normative regulation of these exports were unsuccessful from the viewpoint of both the trade balance and the state budget. A regulation system was introduced in 1985 and was partly changed in the beginning of 1988. It was based on the following principles (Nagy 1988, pp. 128–29; Meisel et al. 1988), most of which had also characterized the former system:

(1) The necessity of increasing ruble exports was evaluated on a

case-by-case basis by the National Planning Board, the Ministry of Foreign Trade, and the Ministry of Finance.

(2) Profits earned by an enterprise from ruble exports were established at the end of each year starting from the difference between incomes from and direct costs of sales on other markets. So enterprises had practically no influence on the development of sales prices on CMEA markets on the microlevel since prices for exports and imports were usually established between the two ministries of foreign trade of the countries trading bilaterally with each other, but these prices had no direct links with prices finally paid or received by the enterprises involved.

(3) Profits from ruble exports could not, in principle, exceed those achieved in other sales, but exceptional treatment in cases where stimulation of ruble exports was judged necessary by the authorities was not ruled out.

(4) Direct costs of ruble exports could not exceed prices obtained for these sales on the enterprise level.

The system was quite complicated and provided grounds for widespread bargaining. Moreover, it encouraged enterprises to transfer profits earned in ruble exports to other sales in order to diminish eventual levies on profits from ruble exports. The logic of the system required that profitability be relatively high in other sales, with these profitability indicators determining, *ex post*, profitability in ruble exports. So profitability in other sales was often made to appear high artificially. Another weak point of the system, one with inflationary effects, was that price increases in convertible-currency exports and in domestic sales due to inflation almost automatically led to increases in subsidies for ruble exports.

Changes in economic policies had been unable to handle a serious structural weakness of Hungarian foreign trade. The problem of trade conversion between two markets, meaning the conversion of hard-currency imports into ruble exports by the same firm, existed at least until the abolition of the CMEA and its trade system, but it can be surmised that surviving bilateral clearing systems have preserved it to a certain extent (Török 1990).

Exporters and importers were supposed to behave according to completely different market patterns in convertible currency and nonconvertible currency, i.e., mostly transferable-ruble trade. This led to a difficult situation when an enterprise was a net importer from one type of market and a net exporter to the other. Regulation stimulated ruble imports and convertible-currency exports. A microlevel linkage between them was common in the petrochemical and the iron and steel industries, i.e., the structurally weakest sectors of industry in Hungary.

These stimulation efforts, however, had an effect counterproductive to structural change. They also led to increasing ruble exports. This increase, first of all in machinery, clothing, and other light industries and in agriculture, was conditioned on a further increase in convertible-currency exports through the opposite mechanism, i.e., convertible-currency imports–ruble exports, in a sort of vicious circle. This mechanism increased the nominal or structural openness, as measured by the export-to-GDP ratio, of the economy toward both markets but had clear consequences in worsening the overall and the marginal profitability of foreign trade.

The mechanism described above was valid mostly for big state firms in the so-called smokestack industries. Therefore, some of them were not really interested in serious reforms of the foreign-trade system, since they could profit well enough from the economy's relative isolation from the capitalist world market. But the gradual liberalization of the foreign-trade system gained speed from 1985 on, and the process was accomplished in six or seven years.

In the first important development, between 1985 and 1988, all productive enterprises became free to engage in foreign trade. A regulation implemented in 1988 made the growth of convertible-currency imports a function of export growth for all enterprises. The unexpected success of this system, causing the volume of nonruble exports to increase by 12.2 percent while the volume of nonruble imports declined by 2.8 percent in 1988, persuaded the government that the liberalization of convertible-currency imports could also be beneficial for the trade balance if aggregate domestic demand could be kept under control by means of monetary policy. Therefore the import-licensing system was abolished in 1989 for most engineering goods and consumer durables, but an import-deposit scheme was also introduced. The share of imported items not liable to licensing was approximately 40 percent in 1989. This percentage increased to 70 percent in 1990 and to 93 percent in 1991. 1991 was the first year without intra-CMEA trade based on the transferable-ruble–based clearing system, and this was also the first year when the new tariff-based protection system was operational. There were no taxes or other financial charges on exports, the average level of customs duties on imports was down from 16 percent to 13 percent, but a new regulatory tool meant to contain consumer-goods imports came into full effect. The aggregate amount of the so-called global quotas had reached only USD 200 million in 1990, and it was far from comprehensive. Its scope was extended and its global amount increased to USD 630 million in 1991.

The sweeping changes in the regulation of foreign trade made the Hungarian market essentially an open one for imports. This process was accomplished exactly at the time when the intra-CMEA trading system collapsed and the contraction of the domestic market made life for domestic producers hard anyway. Therefore, sharply increasing import competition hit many Hungarian industrial firms at a time when their traditional CMEA and domestic markets began to disappear or dwindle. The fact that external shocks were not spread out over time made many enterprises very vulnerable to the microeconomic impacts of the transition process.

The acceleration of privatization exacerbated these market losses for quite a few firms in such industries as consumer electronics, clothing, footwear, and white household goods in a quite special way. In these sectors, foreign investors had the acquisition of domestic distribution channels as a priority. Therefore, the access of these Hungarian producers to domestic market outlets was reduced by the ownership change of their wholesaler or retailer partners, and the newly privatized and now foreign-owned retail chains became a gateway for otherwise not-so-competitive imports.

The changes in the competitive environment of Hungarian industrial firms had become dramatic by 1990. These changes took place in an increasingly austere domestic financial climate, and they introduced a period of severe crisis and partial deindustrialization in Hungarian industry, a topic that we examine in detail in the next chapter.

Chapter 2

Structural Change and Deindustrialization after 1988

Since the economic-policy background of structural developments in industry is known from the previous chapter, this chapter will first outline recent changes in the macrostructure of industry. This dwindling of industry that we describe leads to the question of the role of the state in the restructuring process, with some questions on the possible scope of current industrial policy in Hungary.

2.1 Macrostructural Changes

Indices of output show a marked decline for each sector of Hungarian industry during the period 1988–91 as well as for its last year. This across-the-board decrease is shown by the data in Tables 9 and 10.

The magnitude of the deindustrialization process in Hungary can be seen by comparing 1991 output volume indices, taking the levels of 1987, the last year of growth, as 100. The decrease in the volume of output was 28.3 percent in mining, 5.7 percent in the electric-energy industry, 40.6 percent in metallurgy, 45.3 percent in engineering, 36.4 percent in the building-materials industry, 24.9 percent in the chemicals industry, 26.7 percent in light industry, 11.9 percent in the food industry, and 29.4 percent for industry as a whole.

These sectoral averages might create the impression that Hungarian industry as such has collapsed. This is not true, and some subsectoral figures show how the overall picture has been changing on lower levels of the structure. Metallurgy is a sector where, to begin with, the main subsectors have performed in divergent ways. Iron and steel, for example, was able to defend itself from mounting structural pressures

Table 9

Indices of Volume of Output by Sectors of Hungarian Industry
(1988–91, previous year = 100)

SECTOR	1988	1989	1990	1991
Mining	96.3	94.8	88.2	89.1
Electric Energy	100.1	102.2	100.2	92.0
Metallurgy	104.3	104.4	81.0	67.3
Engineering	100.0	100.2	83.8	65.1
Building material	101.6	98.4	95.0	67.0
Chemicals	101.3	96.1	94.6	81.5
Light Industry	100.2	95.2	88.3	75.1
Food Industry	97.5	101.0	99.1	90.3
Industry Total	100.0	99.0	90.8	78.5

Source: *Statisztikai Havi Közlemények*, 1992, no. 4. KSH, Budapest, April 1992, pp. 20–24.

Note: These figures raise serious methodological problems that cannot be tackled here in detail. Our source indicated that data series from 1989 on include only firms with 50 employees or more. This means creating time series from these figures would be impossible. To give just one reason: in the case of firms transformed and later privatized in a holding-based structure, all the subsidiaries below the critical employment level would disappear from the statistics even if they remained part of the same enterprise group. But our source implies these differences should still remain close to insignificant. For example, it says the volume index of total industrial output including all firms would be 80.9 instead of 78.5 for 1991. Our personal estimate is that this 80.9 figure is far too low and should be situated in the 90–93 range.

Table 10

Sales of Hungarian Industry, January 1991–February 1992 (constant prices)

	monthly average of 1985 = 100													
	1991 Jan.	**1991 Feb.**	**1991 March**	**1991 Apr.**	**1991 May**	**1991 June**	**1991 July**	**1991 Aug.**	**1991 Sept.**	**1991 Oct.**	**1991 Nov.**	**1991 Dec.**	**1992 Jan.**	**1992 Feb.**
Mining Industry	77.5	85.0	75.8	76.5	77.2	70.7	72.2	65.9	53.9	60.8	60.0	61.2	61.7	64.2
Elect. Engineering Ind.	104.6	107.2	100.1	101.1	98.8	94.5	89.7	92.9	92.4	93.9	92.7	92.0	93.4	97.5
Metallurgy Industry	74.5	68.3	65.8	85.0	59.1	57.2	53.4	37.7	42.2	42.0	41.5	39.0	32.4	45.8
Engineering Industry	81.8	75.9	47.9	60.4	56.0	51.5	63.9	58.5	41.5	47.7	46.8	44.4	40.0	44.2
Building Material Ind.	78.7	66.8	62.5	67.2	63.3	67.8	70.7	64.0	63.7	60.6	57.0	49.6	60.2	57.5
Chemical Industry	86.8	85.6	84.8	83.5	75.6	72.4	74.3	72.0	68.2	72.1	70.4	69.9	81.8	70.6
Light Industry	77.4	74.1	66.8	68.2	62.6	59.3	61.2	56.6	54.4	54.9	52.7	51.5	53.1	55.0
Miscellaneous Industry	48.9	40.4	25.7	33.6	32.5	41.2	36.0	34.1	25.6	29.0	27.7	26.9	32.6	30.9
Food Processing Ind.	90.4	94.1	90.0	89.3	88.1	87.4	89.3	88.1	89.8	87.9	86.8	78.0	87.7	82.8
INDUSTRY TOTAL	81.6	80.8	75.3	74.6	70.9	68.6	69.1	66.5	64.4	64.0	63.2	61.1	60.9	61.4

before 1990, with its output even increasing by 4.6 percent in the 1987–89 period. But the size of the decrease between 1989 and 1991 was 52.1 percent, with major producers, such as the companies based at Ozd and Diósgyőr, coming very close to disappearing from the market. DIMAG of Diósgyőr definitely stopped production in June 1992, and eventually it could be resuscitated only as some sort of a mini–steel mill.

Engineering has been a field with largely different subsectoral performances, but it is evident that subsectors oriented toward the former CMEA market were hit the worst. In four of these—the vehicles, the electrical-engineering, the telecommunications, and the precision-instruments industries—the loss of output in 1991 alone was between 27.8 percent for electrical engineering and 48.1 percent in precision engineering. Figures for the 1987–91 period—65.0 percent for vehicles, 42.3 percent for electrical engineering, 44.6 percent for telecom equipment, and 44.2 percent for precision instruments—show dramatic losses of output that mean, as a matter of fact, the quasi disappearance of whole industries. To give just one example: in the consumer-electronics field, the two major domestic players on the market, Videoton and Orion, had to declare bankruptcy in 1991 and 1992, and their output went down to almost residual levels. One subsector within engineering, nonelectrical machinery, however, has been able to remain in relatively good condition; its cumulative loss of output volume was 32.6 percent between 1987 and 1991.

The chemical industry is another sector within which strongly divergent patterns of performance can be observed. Two subsectors, the rubber and the fertilizer industries, were almost in a tailspin; loss of output between 1987 and 1991 was 39.2 percent for the former and an astonishing 62.4 percent for the latter. The fertilizer industry registered a 41.2 percent drop in output in 1991 alone. In contrast, both the petroleum-processing and the pharmaceuticals industries performed relatively well, and their output volume decreased only by 22.8 percent and 24.8 percent, respectively. For both industries, 1991, the first year without intra-CMEA barter trade, proved critical, with 30 percent and 31 percent of loss of output in that year alone.

This fact shows that, even for the relatively successful areas of Hungarian industry, 1991 was a year of disaster with a huge loss of market shares in Eastern Europe and also within Hungary due to an overall growth crisis of the economy. But it has to be noted here that even a subsector's output decline does not necessarily prove that it is in crisis. The good performance of the pharmaceuticals industry is shown by an array of successful privatization deals, such as the partial purchase of Chinoin by Sanofi of France, where the final value of acquisition will depend on profitability achieved in the interim by the joint venture that is still under Hungarian majority ownership.

Our overview of 25 subsectors of Hungarian industry is quite instructive in this respect: there was only one subsector, the brewing industry, with some (1.5 percent) growth in 1991. This was also the only subsector with growth over the period 1987–91.

Light industry has been a crisis sector even more than industry in general. Subsectors suffering the most were the textile industry, the leather, fur, and shoe industries, and the clothing industry, with falls in output between 1987 and 1991 of 44.1 percent, 50.8 percent, and 29.9 percent, respectively. The food industry could be considered almost a success story in this rather grim context. Even the worst performers here, the poultry and the dairy industries, suffered losses of output of only 13.8 percent and 21.2 percent.

The growth picture of Hungarian industry is very clearly that of rapidly shrinking production across the board, with several subsectors where more than half of output has disappeared since 1987 or, in some cases, just in 1990 and 1991. As Tables 11 and 12 show, the employment situation has been even less encouraging, although this also means efficiency has gone up somewhat. The loss of overall industrial employment in 1991 was 16.5 percent, while overall industrial output dropped by 14 percent. Absolute figures show more poignantly the human side of the deindustrialization process: in 1991 alone, the vehicle industry lost 10,200 of 48,800 employees; the precision-instruments industry, 6,100 of 25,100; the telecommunications industry, 14,000 of 53,100; the textile industry, 13,700 of 54,300; and even the only engine of growth, the brewery industry, had to part with 600 of its 8,500 employees. Industry as a whole lost 143,200 of its 888,800 employment between January and December 1991.

The productivity picture has been more than contradictory in Hungarian industry. One might have expected improving productivity as a supply-side response to the crisis, but in most industries declining productivity has been the case, as Table 13 indicates. It is interesting that mining was the only exception, with productivity increases in 1989, 1990, and 1991 as well. Thus, the whole of industry had to struggle with a loss of productivity: average productivity in industry

Table 11

Employment in Hungarian Industry, 1980–91 (thousands)

	1980	1981	1982	1983	1984	1985	1986	1987	1988	1989	1990	1991
Mining Industry	115	114	113	113	112	115	115	112	103	93	78	65
Electrical Engineering Ind.	36	35	35	38	39	39	41	42	43	42	44	41
Metallurgy Industry	97	93	87	82	82	85	87	83	79	72	64	51
Engineering Industry	517	504	498	475	468	482	481	469	460	442	422	318
Building Material Industry	79	77	74	71	70	70	67	65	62	61	59	50
Chemical Industry	110	109	107	106	108	110	111	110	108	110	110	95
Light Industry	409	398	380	364	356	352	345	331	318	303	283	232
Miscellaneous Industry	54	53	51	45	44	42	38	36	32	29	24	17
Food Processing Industry	197	195	195	194	199	201	201	207	203	204	199	181
INDUSTRY TOTAL	1614	1578	1540	1488	1478	1496	1486	1454	1408	1356	1282	1050

Table 12

Employment in Hungarian Industry, January 1991–February 1992 (thousands)

	1991 Jan.	1991 Feb.	1991 March	1991 Apr.	1991 May	1991 June	1991 July	1991 Aug.	1991 Sept.	1991 Oct.	1991 Nov.	1991 Dec.	1992 Jan.	1992 Feb.
Mining Industry	67,5	67,0	66,7	65,4	62,9	62,5	62,1	62,7	61,9	61,0	60,1	58,6	52,6	52,0
Elect. Engineering Ind.	41,2	40,1	40,7	39,1	40,1	39,1	38,7	38,8	38,6	38,6	38,4	38,1	39,5	40,1
Metallurgy Industry	53,2	52,7	48,0	47,9	47,2	46,1	44,8	44,1	43,1	42,3	42,1	41,3	45,2	45,0
Engineering Industry	263,9	257,0	254,6	248,4	242,2	232,5	226,7	221,0	216,7	211,3	206,4	201,7	274,3	271,1
Building Material Ind.	45,7	46,7	45,3	44,4	43,3	41,7	41,5	40,5	39,2	38,0	36,8	36,0	43,2	42,5
Chemical Industry	83,8	84,8	83,7	82,5	81,8	83,7	80,4	80,1	79,3	77,2	76,8	86,2	105,0	104,5
Light Industry	161,7	161,8	160,4	156,3	151,6	147,1	143,7	141,7	142,0	139,5	137,4	135,0	210,4	210,1
Miscellaneous Industry	5,4	5,8	5,5	5,3	6,0	5,7	5,1	5,4	5,6	5,5	4,9	5,0	14,7	14,5
Food Processing Ind.	166,4	165,5	163,6	161,8	160,4	159,3	158,9	157,7	158,5	157,3	155,8	153,7	171,7	169,9
INDUSTRY TOTAL	888,8	881,4	868,5	851,1	835,5	817,7	802,5	792,0	784,9	770,7	758,7	745,6	956,6	949,7

Table 13

Real Output per Worker in Hungarian Industry, 1989–91 (previous year = 100)

	1989	1990	1991
Mining Industry	103.0	106.7	106.0
Elect. Engineering Ind.	103.3	97.3	97.1
Metallurgy Industry	113.6	98.8	82.5
Engineering Industry	101.6	92.3	78.3
Building Material Ind.	100.2	99.6	76.8
Chemical Industry	93.9	98.6	87.9
Light Industry	95.5	98.1	86.8
Miscellaneous Industry	98.0	97.7	86.0
Food Processing Ind.	100.8	102.5	97.2
INDUSTRY TOTAL	100.7	99.6	90.6

improved by 0.7 percent in 1989, declined by 0.4 percent in 1990, and also decreased by 9.4 percent in 1991. Average productivity losses of more than 20 percent in 1991 alone were registered in the engineering and the construction-materials industry, and the decline was above 10 percent in the iron and steel, chemical, and light industries.

The causes of the dramatic overall productivity decline in Hungarian industry have not yet been thoroughly analyzed. Only sporadic material is available from enterprise-level interviews. This material is not sufficient to give an exhaustive list of the causes, nor can their order of importance be established, but a few causes can be enumerated with some explanations, on the condition that they are not taken as definitive before they are confirmed by an appropriately thorough analysis.

The declining trend of investment has resulted in a dramatic undercapitalization of many industrial firms. The share of gross fixed investment in GDP decreased from 28.8 percent in 1980 to 17.8 percent in 1990, within which the share of industry has also declined. Its average share in the volume of gross fixed investment in Hungary was 35.4 percent in the period 1976–80, was 31.7 percent in the next five-year period, and dropped to 29.0 percent in 1986–90 (Friss 1992, pp. 9–10). Loss-making production is maintained in an array of state firms where privatization is yet to be undertaken. This can be explained by the uncertainty about the interests of the owner and how they are to be protected. Managers of many loss-making firms use up the firm's assets to cover current losses because their strategic priority is the survival of the enterprise at almost any price. This asset-subtracting attitude (cf., Török 1992) will continue to prevail in a significant part of Hungarian industry unless the management of state-owned assets is not reassuringly taken care of on a mass scale. A partial solution to this problem might be provided by the government with the creation of the State Asset Management Corporation (SAMC).

Productivity losses are also the consequence of a fierce competition for market share. Former productivity figures for many Hungarian sectors or firms have to be understood with respect to the oligopolistic or even monopolistic character of their protected domestic and CMEA markets before, and also partly in, 1990. An increasingly massive demand-side squeeze on sales prices has been the case for most Hungarian industrial firms in recent years, with obvious implications for productivity.

Employment and productivity trends imply that the employment consequences of the crisis have been less dramatic in many cases than the decline in output. This has been a result of a special type of enterprise strategy observable in many Hungarian firms; it has been analyzed by several authors (Török 1991; Erdős 1991; Laki 1992). We can call this a strategy of drifting, which means that enterprises in crisis do not invest on a large scale due to their liquidity and debt problems but most of them are hesitant to lay off labor. Their main concern is short-term survival, with the only hope of a long-term resolution of their problems being the fact that many firms face a similar situation. The simultaneous collapse of many firms cannot be allowed by the government, and thus some sort of bailout must be in the offing—at least this is the most frequent rationale for deliberate drifting.

2.2 The Options of Industrial Policy

We have shown that Hungarian industry went through a period of crisis in 1990 and, even more, in 1991. The government did not take any measures of significance to stop the process of the shrinking of industry. It only intervened in a few sectors where the explosion of unemployment threatened serious political consequences, but most of these interventions had a strictly regional and temporary character.

Hungarian industrial policy was less and less interventionist from 1985 on, and quite a few goals of the immediately pre-1990 industrial policy were accepted by the industrial policy makers of the new, freely elected government. Such common goals were privatization, the liberalization of competition across borders and within them, and the creation of a well-functioning system of R&D financing for promising projects or firms.

Despite the apparent similarities between their objectives, the industrial-policy tasks of the new government had dimensions different in scope and in size from those of its predecessor. These differences are linked to the much larger extent of privatization, to the new challenges arising from the almost-complete liberalization of imports, and to the definition of industrial policy itself, with all its implications for the reallocation of resources for industry's R&D purposes.

Privatization remained a major responsibility of industrial policy, but the creation of the State Property Agency (SPA) in early 1990 made it clear that no former ministry would be given the task of coordinating and carrying out privatization policy as a whole. The Ministry of Industry and Trade has had a rather special role in the transformation and privatization of industrial enterprises: it has been acting as the founder of state firms in industry or trade, but not as the owner of their assets. Its basic task in this regard consists of strategic control over management through the reelected boards of supervision. These boards also helped to prepare enterprises for privatization, but they mostly had only one vote or two out of seven or nine when major privatization decisions were taken with the active participation of the SPA.

The role of the ministry in competition policy has been similar. It was just one voice among many from the government when major issues of import protection or fair competition were discussed. The main role here has belonged to the Office of Competition, a successor of the defunct Office of Prices and Materials.

Therefore, the allocative and structural-policy functions of industrial policy could have come to the forefront. These functions, however, needed major clarifications. They could be performed only in the framework of a consistent industrial policy from which any tool allowing for interventionism had to be excluded. This has been a very hard constraint, but it has been adhered to:

• for obvious political reasons linked to suspicions as far as any sort of political restoration of the former regime disguised as centralization were concerned;

• due to the overall liberalization of the economy; and

• owing to privatization, which stripped the government of the possibility of direct control over an increasing part of the enterprise sphere.

These constraints threatened to downgrade industrial policy to the role of management and coordination of strategic resources and sectors of industry. Therefore, the need for formulating a new industrial policy became imminent. The strategy document outlining the new industrial-policy thinking of the Hungarian government was prepared by the team of Minister Peter Akos Bod in 1991. It attempted to make clear that the constraint of nonintervention was meant to be put in conformity with an active role of industrial policy in picking winners, as modern industrial policies in Western Europe do. The basic idea of this strategy is that industrial policy has to influence the microsphere directly. The document gives only very general guidelines for sectoral structural policies, and it emphasizes the role of the state in orienting resource flows toward promising products, technologies, or enterprises. Therefore, the new strategy mix has very few sector-specific targets or tools, and it almost completely abandons the traditional macro approach of former Hungarian industrial policies.

This strategy document was quite well received by the Hungarian scientific and industrial communities, but its realization was hampered by unexpected developments. A wave of bankruptcies and deep financial crises swept through big state firms of the metallurgy, motor-vehicles, and electronics industries, and crisis management became the foremost task of industrial policy makers. The already-mentioned noninterventionist stance of industrial policy seems to have had some institutional consequences in this respect. The Ministry of Industry and Trade does not have any significant financial resources to help restructure big state firms. This is why it has had to perform the role of mediator between managements, banks, and the Ministry of Finance. So it really could not take any major step forward in implementing its well-formulated industrial strategy focusing upon those fields of Hungarian industry that would be the most able to integrate into European and world industry.

Chapter 3

Firms in Crisis and Transition

3.1 Overview

This chapter and the two following it examine the behavior of Hungarian enterprises during 1991–92. The findings are based on interviews with six Hungarian firms:

- Budaprint, a state-owned textile enterprise;
- Gedeon Richter, a state-owned pharmaceutical firm in the process of being privatized;
- the Hungarian National Oil and Gas Trust, an integrated energy firm in the process of being reorganized for privatization;
- Müszertechnika, a privately owned firm engaged in the manufacture of computers and electrical equipment;
- Szim, a state-owned firm in the machine-tools sector; and
- Taurus, a state-owned firm producing tires and rubber products.

These firms encompass a broad range of problems and characteristics typical of Hungarian industry. Thus, we believe that relatively broad interpretations and conclusions can be drawn from these case studies.

As a further test of the validity of the case-study approach as a tool for investigating the effects of the transition from socialism to capitalism on East European firms, each of our respondent firms was interviewed twice, the first time in January 1991 and the second time in the spring and summer of 1992. The earlier set of interviews was written up before the reinterviews were carried out, and interview summaries and conclusions drawn from them are reported in this chapter and the next without updating. This affords the reader an opportunity to compare our evaluations and prognostications based on the earlier set of interviews with what actually happened to the firms in the following year or so. Thus the reader should be able to form some impression of the utility of enterprise-level interviews as a tool for analysis and forecasting in a relatively turbulent environment.

Because the firms in this sample were strongly influenced by domestic and foreign shocks, we precede the case studies with a description of the economic and policy environment in 1991–92 and draw some general conclusions from the interviews. These conclusions are further refined after presentation of the interviews and their updates.

3.2 The Domestic Economic Environment and Enterprise Behavior

There were three principal impulses from the domestic economy that influenced enterprise behavior during the period under review. The first was the effect of the government's tight monetary policy, which acted to reduce aggregate demand, to force many enterprises to rely on interenterprise debt rather than on bank credit, and to hamper restructuring efforts of enterprises by making it difficult to obtain funds required to cut costs of production and to change product lines. The second effect was a decline in aggregate demand, which made itself felt either in a reduced demand within Hungary for the output of the firms interviewed or in an increased degree of price competition and reduced profit margins on domestic sales. Finally, firms began to perceive the emergence of a new regulatory regime, one where they would face harder budget constraints and be required to make strategic decisions with less influence from government authorities.

Macroeconomic Conditions and Policies in Hungary

The macroeconomic policy stance has basically remained the same during the last ten years or so. The top priority has been restrictive demand management in order to accelerate structural change in the economy and to maintain Hungary's ability to service foreign debt. From one year to another, though, quite significant shifts occurred among other important macroeconomic priorities, such as export performance, balance of payments, inflation, and the budget deficit.

An improving or altogether good export performance during the last two or three years put the other priorities higher on the list. This does not necessarily mean that these other "especially targeted" macroeconomic variables always showed the necessary improvement. For example, even if combating inflation has been one of the arguments the government used in order to justify monetary restrictions and the gradual withdrawal of the state from financial commitments linked to social and educational policies, the rate of inflation has been steadily increasing during the last few years. Whereas its rate did not reach 30 percent per annum in 1990, consumer prices increased by 35.6 percent between January–September 1990 and January–September 1991 (*KSH Täjëkoztató*, November 15, 1991).

Another example, now in a positive sense, of the relative inefficiency of monetary and fiscal policies in influencing macroeconomic developments was the unexpectedly low budget deficit in 1990—HUF 1.4 billion instead of the HUF 9.9 billion planned for that year—which occurred due to surprisingly high corporate tax revenues collected at the end of the year.

If the efficiency of monetary policy is measured by monetary growth, then Hungarian monetary policy can be considered satisfactory. The growth of M2 has remained somewhat below that of the GDP deflator in 1990 and 1991, by –0.8 percent in 1990, and by approximately –0.3 percent in January–September 1991. The increase in interest rates came to a halt after the first quarter of 1991, and they seem to have stabilized, short-term rates at 35 percent per annum, although several experts think this has occurred due to such exceptionally favorable seasonal or exogenous effects as good crops, almost no increases in fuel prices, etc. Nevertheless, we have no reason to underestimate the favorable impacts of tight monetary policy. It is undoubtedly more than just an impression that Hungarian entrepreneurs, enterprises, state institutions, and households complain about the increasing scarcity of money. This is reflected by the fact that black-market exchange rates of convertible currencies have not exceeded official rates by more than 5 percent since the summer of 1990.

The budget situation changed for the worse in 1991. Although the forecast of the 1991 budget deficit was HUF 78 billion, it exceeded HUF 100 billion and 5 percent of the GDP after reaching 3.5 percent in 1989 and practically 0 percent in 1990. This is due mostly to the collapse of exports to Eastern Europe, a 5-percent decrease in household consumption, and a 15-percent fall in the volume of gross industrial output.

The changes in the macroeconomic situation during 1991 point to the strong commitment of the government to keep monetary developments and the external balance under strict control at the expense of the entrepreneurial sector and households. The decrease in GDP, –7 percent as compared to –4 percent in 1990; in domestic absorption, –7 percent as compared to –5 percent in 1990; in gross fixed investment, –12 percent as compared to –6.3 percent in 1990; in household consumption, –5 percent as compared to –4 percent in 1990; and in gross industrial output at constant prices, –15 percent as compared to –8.5 percent in 1990 (forecasts from *KOPINT Report*, 1991, no. 3 [November], p. 72) with the annual CPI up by 35 percent from 29 percent in 1990 are all signs of a deepening recession. But the other side of the coin is that exports were down by only 5 percent from the 1990 level and the balance of payments deficit was only USD 300–400 million, less than half the forecast by the government in early 1991.

All the developments surveyed here show that the Hungarian economy has suffered a minor shock as compared to Poland, which is undergoing a really drastic shock therapy. Hungary's future development depends largely on how well the government can introduce incentives to spur productive investment and to speed up privatization, but it seems quite clear that not the entire productive sphere will need to be rebuilt from scratch.

Effects of Declining Domestic Demand

All firms interviewed reported that domestic demand for their product had either declined or, in the case of Müszertechnika and Gedeon Richter, that the profitability of domestic sales had fallen because of increased competition in the case of the former firm and rising costs and fixed domestic prices of output in the case of the latter. Since the firms in the sample tended to export 60–80 percent of their production, the decline in domestic demand alone would not be a serious problem. However, when combined with import competition and the decline in sales to the former CMEA area, the total decline in demand has represented a significant shock for all the firms with the possible exception of Müszertechnika and Gedeon Richter, who managed to retain much of their former CMEA markets, principally due to unique circumstances. A second source of changes in demand for some firms was the liberalization of prices in Hungary and the elimination of subsidies for food and energy. These relative price changes had two effects. One was to alter the pattern of consumer demand away from food and such basic consumer goods as textiles in the case of Budaprint. The other effect was to raise the prices of energy and energy-intensive inputs.

Finally, some firms, such as Szim and Taurus, had domestic deliveries that were tied to the exports of other Hungarian firms, the exports of buses by the Hungarian bus maker Ikarus in the case of these two firms. In this way, what was a foreign-trade shock for Ikarus from its loss of sales on the former CMEA markets appears as a decline in domestic sales for Szim and Taurus. Thus the operation of the so-called foreign-trade multiplier is evident in this cascade of declining demand.

Effects of Monetary Policy

In 1990 and 1991, the government pursued a tight monetary policy for three reasons. One was to prevent the price increases caused by the elimination of food and energy subsidies from evolving into a self-sustaining inflationary spiral. The second objective was to restrain aggregate demand in a period when the import regime was being liberalized. The third objective was to promote a restructuring of industry by means of a tight-money policy that would force inefficient firms to improve their performance or to go bankrupt. The first two objectives, largely macroeconomic in nature, appear to have been achieved. The last objective, largely microeconomic, appears, based on our interviews, to have been only partially fulfilled at best.

The tight-money policy has had two additional consequences. One is a lack of long-term capital for the restructuring of enterprises. The other is an explosion of interenterprise debt. Under the old system of payments in Hungary, firms needed little in the way of working capital. Payments for their products were settled through the State Bank within a period of days, or weeks in the case of sales to CMEA customers; only in the case of sales to the West were normal commercial terms with longer payment terms used. Even in the latter case, however, the National Bank of Hungary advanced forint payments against payments of hard currency due from foreign buyers.

The queuing, or involuntary-interenterprise-debt, problem arose already in the two-tiered banking system introduced in early 1987. Payments between enterprises had been settled through their respective merchant banks, and the queuing problem originated as the result of a very severe, sudden, and, moreover, partly retroactive credit crunch in early 1988. It is suspected by prominent experts that queuing is far from being only a result of liquidity problems of loss-making firms that would face bankruptcy in a market economy. Even some profitable enterprises do not pay their bills or pay them with considerable delays, using their portfolio of bank accounts in different banks. These companies simply use this sort of cheap debt as a substitute for expensive bank debt.

The banking reform left the financing of Hungarian enterprises to newly created commercial banks; then, when monetary policy imposed tight lending limits on the banks, firms found themselves with insufficient capital to finance day-to-day purchases of inputs. This appears to be true for both the profitable and the unprofitable firms interviewed. A not atypical result of this situation was the respondent firm whose sales in 1990 fell by 20 percent but whose receivables and payables doubled despite a profitable year. Payment delays of 30 to 90 days and more beyond the due date were often reported, and, given the high rates of inflation in Hungary until very recently, not only a lack of liquidity but also economic self-interest acted to induce even profitable firms to stretch payment terms wherever possible. Moreover, Gedeon Richter, which was continuing to export pharmaceuticals to the USSR, also reported payment delays from that country as well as from the Hungarian government.

Indeed, only the private firm, among the firms interviewed, appears not to have suffered a serious degradation of its balance sheet due to overdue payments. Its managers did acknowledge delays in payments from Hungarian state-owned firms, but for this firm such delays were manageable. This was partly due to the fact that, because the firm was private, it did not have access to government credits in the past and thus had to maintain an adequate level of working capital in the pre–tight-money period. Second, its dealings with the state sector in Hungary were a small part of its business. Finally, it may also be that because it was a private firm, state-owned firms tended to pay their obligations to it more promptly because it was not party to the tacit agreement among state-owned firms to accept payment delays.

The responses of the firms did not suggest that the growth of inter-enterprise debt and the shortage of working capital hampered production by restricting their ability to purchase inputs. In this regard, it was only in the case of imported inputs, where payment could not be delayed, that managers expressed any concerns, but all firms in our sample that raised concerns about short-term liquidity were able to allocate funds for needed imports. Nevertheless, there is some possibility that the easier payments terms on the domestic market relative to imported inputs led to some otherwise uneconomic import substitution by Hungarian enterprises.

While managers were not excessively concerned about the effects of growing interenterprise debt on production, all of them were to various degrees concerned about its financial implications for their firms. Some firms, such as Gedeon Richter, viewed the accumulation of short-term assets of dubious quality as making the privatization of the firm more difficult since such assets would make the firm less attractive to foreign investors. Other firms also voiced concerns about the likelihood that some of the firms to which they had extended credit would not be able to pay their debts.

Despite these concerns, there was very little interest among managers of the state-owned firms in refusing to sell to customers who could not pay promptly. Similarly, the attitude of many managers was that the only way to rectify the problem would be to expand greatly the amount of credit available from the banking sector.

The lack of credit and the inability to raise additional funds in other ways appeared to be influencing the behavior of the state-owned firms in terms of restructuring. Many reported a lack of funds for capital investments that were viewed as vital for changing production in order to become more competitive on domestic or Western markets. It should also be assumed that expenses associated with the maintenance of equipment and buildings were suffering as well. The inability to raise money domestically may also have played an important role in influencing Hungarian firms to seek Western firms as joint-venture partners or as possible investors because these were the most obvious, and perhaps the only, ways to tap Western capital.

The ability to create capital by not paying short-term obligations was also hampering the restructuring of the Hungarian economy, according to some respondents, because it enabled loss-making firms to avoid bankruptcy, thus forestalling the movement of resources to more productive sectors. Managers of firms that were either unprofitable or losing money tended to take another view. First, they pointed to the fact that considerable restructuring and downsizing of their firms had taken place (see, for example, the Budaprint and Szim cases), and restructuring was continuing, at times in the face of political opposition.

Second, they argued that much of their firm's long-term debt had been incurred as part of previous government-organized restructurings or injections of capital designed to make the firms viable. Indeed, this attitude that enterprise long-term debt had been arbitrarily and somewhat randomly imposed on firms and that it represented obligations that reflected past decisions of a now-discredited political system was widespread among our respondents. Thus, managers were resentful of having to deal with long-term debt repayment obligations and at the same time somewhat fatalistic about the situation of heavily indebted firms. They were attempting to meet their long-term debt obligations, but it appeared that the servicing and repayment of long-term debt had the lowest claim on enterprise funds. In part this may reflect the above-mentioned belief that enterprises had little moral responsibility for these debts, but other factors may be important as well. Among these are a belief that banks will not take action against enterprises unable to service their loans; uncertainty regarding the long-term creditability of the hard-budget, tight-money policy; and the fact that the Hungarian capital market offers no useful means of refinancing firms in a way that would make debt repayment easier. Thus servicing the debt out of operating profits, if these exist, is the only option for many firms.

The danger of this situation is that because these old debts are somewhat arbitrarily distributed among enterprises by past government investment policies, some firms that would prove profitable if unburdened by their debt will fail even if they can operate profitably in terms of current revenues and expenses because they will lack the cash flow needed to service their debt. Moreover, the enterprise sector as a whole may prove to be cash starved and unable to provide sufficient investment funds for restructuring and technical renovation.

3.3 International Economic Environment

All enterprises in our sample save the National Oil and Gas Trust depend on foreign markets for 60–80 percent of their sales. Exports tended to be equally divided between Western markets and the former CMEA countries. With the economic collapse of the Soviet and East European economies and the reunification of Germany, sales to the CMEA countries declined in 1990, and the decline continued in 1991 with the breakdown of the CMEA and the reversion of its members to trade at world market prices and payments in convertible currencies.

Policy Measures and Recent Developments

The list of import items subject to liberalization has reached 90 percent of all items of commodities imported. The impacts of liberalization have been clearly positive in creating a competitive domestic market environment. Liberalization of imports had to be accompanied by restrictive demand management in order to avoid the collapse of import-competing producers and of the trade balance. Even so, a few sectors, such as consumer electronics, have almost completely disappeared due to import competition that increased abruptly, leaving Hungarian producers no opportunity for a "soft landing." Other domestic producers who complain that they are unable to compete with foreign producers' aggressive sales policies supported by large marketing budgets are those selling detergents, textiles, building materials, and shoes. Another important fact is that the Hungarian customs-duties system, with an average tariff rate of 13 percent, is supported by only a few of the nontariff barriers (NTBs) commonly used in industrialized market countries.

The annual growth of convertible-currency exports was 12.3 percent in 1988, 5.0 percent in 1989, and 9.5 percent in 1990. The comparable figure for all exports will be –5 to –6 percent in 1991. Convertible-currency imports declined by 2.8 percent in 1988 and increased by 7.1 percent in 1989 and by 2.8 percent in 1990. The comparable figure for all imports for 1991 is between 0 and 1 percent.

Terms of trade were 102.4 in 1988, 102.8 in 1989, and 100.4 in 1990. The KOPINT forecast for 1991 was 88.0. This deterioration is due mainly to a sharp increase in import prices of oil, gas, etc., from the Soviet Union due to the conversion to payments in dollars. The trade balance in convertible-currency trade in 1990 was USD 687 million; for January–September 1991 it was USD –1,378 million, out of which USD –550 million was with the Soviet Union.

Vis-à-vis the West, the most important policy measure was the liberalization of import restrictions so that by 1991 less than 10 percent of imports required licenses. This was achieved without creating a hard-currency deficit, and trade liberalization appears to have had positive effects on competition and on input supplies on the domestic market.

Trade with the former CMEA countries fell in 1991 in large part because Soviet enterprises lacked the hard currency to purchase Hungarian goods. In the case of Gedeon Richter, exports of pharmaceuticals to the USSR continued because these were purchased by a Soviet trading company with centrally allocated foreign exchange. In the case of Müszertechnika, sales were based on a scheme of bartering personal computers for Soviet steel, a process legal in the USSR only because the parties to the barter process were engaged in a joint venture. In addition to declining demand, the interest of some Hungarian exporters in the CMEA market has been reduced by administrative measures, including a 30 percent tax on exports cleared in rubles.

Trade Relations with the West

Perhaps the most favorable development mentioned by firms was that Hungary's import liberalization made it easy to import equipment and components from the West without undue delay. Of course, since firms could not delay payments on imports in the way that they could on domestic purchases, liquidity constraints limited respondents' ability to import from the West. A number of firms, including Müszertechnika in computers and Budaprint in textiles, indicated greater market competition from imports, including an increased market share for foreign producers and lower prices as the result of price competition.

All firms in the sample were attempting to increase sales to Western markets. Some, such as Taurus, which had received support from the World Bank for a consulting study of its market position, were engaged in long-term measures to alter their technology and products so as to make them more competitive on Western markets. However, the principal response to the need to expand sales to the West was to seek out joint-venture partners. In part this was a response to the relatively weak marketing network that most Hungarian firms have in the West. Taurus has perhaps the strongest distribution network, but none of the firms interviewed had a strong structure of affiliates, subsidiaries, warehousing, or production operations or even sales offices in Western countries. Thus the extent to which exporting was used to penetrate foreign markets is much greater than would be the case in Western firms of comparable size and dependence on foreign markets. Joint ventures are seen as a means for overcoming this structural weakness quickly and without the need to expend resources to develop foreign sales, service, and production networks or to await the trained international business specialists that such a strategy would require.

Trade with the Former CMEA

Because the USSR played a pivotal role in Hungary's exports to the CMEA region, the developments of 1990 and 1991 had a particularly severe impact on Hungarian enterprises. With a few exceptions, such as Müszertechnika and Gedeon Richter, most respondents expected no exports to the USSR in the first half of 1991 and only several had some faint hopes that they could begin to export to the USSR in the second half of 1991 or by 1992 at the latest. On the Soviet market, the difficulty was that Soviet importing firms were required to pay in hard currency for their imports from Hungary and often had no access to this means of payment. Managers of several firms said that there was a significant demand for their products in the USSR, and they hoped that barter arrangements or some nondollar form of clearing could be arranged.

Possibilities for the improvement of the volume of exports to the successor republics of the USSR are mixed. On the one hand, the Hungarian government appears not to want to extend credits for the financing of exports to these new states, nor is it especially anxious to allow an extensive barter trade with them to reemerge on the assumption that such trade would slow down the restructuring of industry and help perpetuate the dual-sector nature of Hungarian industry (one for exports to the West, the other for exports to the USSR). At the same time, knowledgeable respondents in Hungary reported that the devolution of central power in the USSR to newly independent republics has already given rise to a significant volume of barter trade between Hungary and those republics, such as Ukraine, that are sufficiently close to Hungary and have something to barter. What the true volume of this trade might be and what its significance is for the firms in our sample could not be determined. Nevertheless, the payments difficulties of the former USSR and the weakening of central authority in that country suggest that barter arrangements may have some useful role to play in restoring Hungarian trade with the region.

3.4 Corporate Restructuring Strategies

Both Hungary's foreign-trade and macroeconomic policies and the shock from the collapse of CMEA trade served as an important impetus for the restructuring of Hungarian industry. Restructuring involves a wide range of activities and possibilities for Hungarian firms. First, it is to be understood that any restructuring activities entail a decreased dependence on former CMEA markets and a proportionally larger role for domestic and Western sales. This already raises the question of size, since some firms may not be able to shift products from the East to the West and must therefore reduce output and employment, even to the point of going out of existence. Other firms may wish to expand as their success on the domestic or Western market dictates. A second element of restructuring involves changes in the product profile of individual enterprises as their market focus changes. Such changes in output profile may also be accompanied by changes in the firm's technology. Finally, restructuring may involve changes in the organization of the firm's business operations, for example, by reorganizing management, the legal corporate structure, or the nature of the firm's ownership. Some element of all these restructuring strategies could be discerned among the firms interviewed.

Barriers to Restructuring

Changes in the size of firms is hampered by several factors. The first is that there are formal and informal political and social barriers to laying off workers and shutting down work places. Particularly in the case of firms that operated plants in small towns outside Budapest, where the employment effects of shutdowns would be severe, managers noted that decreases in the work force that were being implemented were often smaller than purely economic factors would dictate, largely in response to government pressure or "expectations" that state-owned firms would do their part to help ease the problem of open unemployment. Firms also reported that tax laws made it less attractive than it might otherwise be to reduce employment, as the financial benefits of reducing the wage bill often accrued to the government rather than to the firm. Nevertheless, a downsizing of the labor force was a very common response, with Taurus, Szim, and Budaprint, for example, all reducing their work forces by significant numbers.

The only firm with appreciable current interest in expanding its operations was Müszertechnika, and the principal barrier appeared to be financial rather than the acquisition of necessary plant or equipment. The firm was planning to sell stock to the public to raise funds for its expansion. It had purchased buildings from a state-owned firm, and an inspection of the facilities suggested that the firm had ample space to expand production at this facility. Gedeon Richter was constrained from expanding its product line, and therefore, conceivably, its overall size, by a lack of funds for bringing new pharmaceuticals to the market. This process is quite expensive, and the firm was unable to obtain R&D funds from the state or the necessary loans from banks to finance these efforts. It is probable that, had the other firms wished to expand their operations in response to market developments, they, too, would have faced few difficulties in obtaining the needed labor, plant, and equipment but considerable, if not insurmountable, difficulties in obtaining the necessary long-term financing for new capital or the short-term credits needed to meet increased working-capital requirements. Firms that have inherited large amounts of long-term debt would be particularly handicapped in efforts to increase their production.

Finally, the concept of bankruptcy was not well understood, nor did it seem a serious possibility to our respondents, although some admitted that some affiliates or plants would prove not to be viable in the long run and have to be closed. Nevertheless, in the immediate future firms neither feared being forced into bankruptcy nor expected to undertake liquidation voluntarily.

Changes in product structure were being undertaken by virtually all firms interviewed, but here, too, numerous obstacles were mentioned by respondents. Financing was a problem for many firms, but perhaps more important were a lack of familiarity with Western market needs and, even more, a conceptual framework for utilizing that knowledge. Firms varied considerably in this respect. For example, Taurus's management appeared to have a good understanding of the global tire market and the firm's role within that market. In part this surely reflected the firm's long-standing involvement in the world market, and such a good knowledge of the global market and the firm's position on this market were also evident among some other respondent firms, such as Gedeon Richter, that had a strong and independent involvement in the Western market. Taurus was also assisted by a study prepared by Western consultants and financed by World Bank funds. As a result, Taurus was able to articulate somewhat more clearly a restructuring of production that was based on a strategic vision of the firm's position on world markets. It must be added that the firm's managers admitted that their restructuring was not wholly up to this strategic vision due to financial and government constraints on Taurus's restructuring efforts.

Other firms were to varying degrees less able to convert their knowledge and current export experience toward the West into a strategic vision of what their competitive advantage was and how it ought to be exploited and nurtured. Evidence of this failure to think about restructuring in a strategic way, a way of charting the firm's future that is common practice among Western firms, was evident in two types of responses regarding the restructuring of products and production. One was the notion, expressed by several respondents, that their firm was seeking better technology, usually in the form of Western machinery, in order to become more competitive. While there is no doubt that better technology would make better products, little thought seems to have been given to which machinery ought to be obtained and for which product lines. More problematic is the fact that injections of new capital to raise productivity reflect the old pattern of restructurings of unprofitable operations practiced by the former regime in Hungary. The Budaprint and Szim cases are telling examples of efforts to make firms more profitable by injecting more productive equipment into the firm. While profits may have gone up in the short run, in the long run they did not cover the true costs of the investment.

A second set of responses that reflected a lack of strategic thinking that would combine market analysis and an understanding of the firm's competitive advantages into an integrated vision for developing production had to do with explanations of actual or anticipated changes in products or technology. Many of these, while perfectly rational and proper under the circumstances, were also entirely *ad hoc*, with no coherent strategic vision behind them. Thus, for example, Budaprint was forced to import cotton from the West; due to the higher quality of this cotton relative to previous supplies from the USSR, the firm moved toward the production of higher-quality fabric. Whether the market situation and the firm's long-term market strategy were consistent with such a decision was not clear. As another example, one of Szim's affiliates was able to obtain a large number of Western orders for computer–numerically controlled machine tools, and thus Szim's management chose to subsidize this affiliate in the hope that it would become profitable. While these are relatively small business decisions, in the end they determine the firm's range of products and technologies; yet there appeared to be little in the way of a strategic vision of what the firm ought to be doing and more of a view that, if it is possible and some argument can be made to do so, then any available course of action ought to be undertaken.

On a larger scale, this lack of strategic vision was evident in the choice of joint-venture partners. In many cases, Hungarian firms appeared to be hoping that a Western firm would turn up as a joint-venture partner in order to enable the Hungarian partner to change the product mix so that it would better penetrate Western markets. Thus Hungarian firms sought as joint-venture partners Western firms that were financially strong and that had good reputations for their technology. Whether the Western firm represented a good fit for the Hungarian firm in terms of the Hungarian partner's own capabilities and strategic objectives seemed of little concern. Moreover, the Hungarian partners in the joint venture appeared more interested in projects that would lead to quick exports and some infusion of capital and technology than in seeking out partnerships that were consistent with their own strategic objectives.

While the decisions of Hungarian firms may prove in the end to have been correct and profitable, there is a danger that the pattern of production of Hungarian firms will reflect more the short-term exigencies and opportunities thrown up by Western markets and joint-venture partners than by the long-term competitive strengths and capabilities of Hungarian firms.

Finally, there is some evidence of the reorganization of the internal structure of firms, much of it toward structures to be found in market economies. Examples include:

—Müszertechnika, which has evolved from a cooperative to a closely held corporation that is now changing to a firm whose shares will be sold to the public;

—Hungarian National Oil and Gas Trust, which is being reorganized into separate production and distribution companies, much along the lines seen in the energy sector of developed market economies;

—Szim and Budaprint are organized in a holding company and affiliate framework to centralize long-term debt management;

—Gedeon Richter is being reorganized as a prelude to privatization.

In these changes, the motivating factors of financial exigencies and impending ownership changes predominate. With the exception of Müszertechnika, there were no major organizational changes being undertaken to reflect the reality of expanded dependence on Western markets better or to increase firms' responsiveness to or competitiveness on Western markets.

Implications for Hungarian Industry

To the extent that the findings of our interviews can be generalized to Hungarian industry at large, several conclusions can be drawn:

1. The collapse of the CMEA market has had a significant impact on the demand for the products of most Hungarian firms. It is difficult to distinguish between the effect of the CMEA collapse and the consequences of a decline in domestic demand, competition from imports, and changes in relative prices, but the CMEA shock appears to be quantitatively the largest impulse acting on Hungarian firms.

2. Hungarian firms are being forced to make adjustments in output and employment, although government policies make it difficult to adjust labor and product profiles as rapidly as firms may wish.

3. Most Hungarian firms are being forced to turn toward Western markets, but their adjustment in this direction is hampered by a lack of capital. However, simply increasing the amount of credit to the Hungarian enterprise sector is unlikely to solve the problem. Due to the existing volume of interenterprise debt, the ability of the Hungarian capital market to distinguish between viable and nonviable firms is limited. Therefore, both potential winners and potential losers are now being starved of credits, but if there were more credits, they would likely also go to both, thus delaying restructuring even more. This is especially true of firms in the state sector.

4. Enterprise adjustments in output volume and mix are generally in the right direction, although constrained by the macroeconomic environment and by policy factors. However, the managers of Hungarian firms are not formulating long-term strategies for their enterprises to the extent that is desirable. The great dependence on the resources of potential Western partners and a faith that infusions of Western technology and know-how are the keys to profitability are leaving the future profile of Hungarian industrial production in considerable part to serendipitous contacts between Western and Hungarian firms.

Chapter 4

Hungarian Enterprise Behavior
Case Studies, 1991

4.1 Taurus

Company Background

Taurus is a large, state-owned enterprise that produces a variety of rubber goods, with tires for trucks and farm equipment accounting for over 50 percent of its total turnover or sales of approximately HUF 20 billion. It employs about 9,000 workers at six factories in Hungary.

Markets

A. Current Market Situation

Of its tire production, over 60 percent is exported, largely to developed and developing market economies, where it is marketed by local sales representatives and offices and by dealers or through state channels in developing countries where state trading is practiced. The technical-rubber division is more dependent on the domestic market, slightly less than 60 percent of sales, and on the CMEA market on the export side. The company also imports tires and other rubber goods, and the resale of these products accounts for 25 percent of the company's turnover.

B. Recent Market Trends

Although over 60 percent of tire production is exported, the actual demand for tires is even more subject to influence from international trade because a large component of domestic sales involves the provision of tires to Ikarus, Hungary's bus manufacturer. With Ikarus's markets in the former CMEA countries disappearing, the domestic demand for Taurus tires has also declined. A further source of demand decline was the reduction of economic activity in Hungary and to a lesser extent in the Western countries to which Taurus exports. These declines in economic activity led to reduced transportation activity and therefore lower demand for replacement tires, which are a mainstay of Taurus's business. At the same time, Taurus has expanded its ability to produce radial truck tires, thus strengthening itself in a growing market segment.

Market Strategies

The firm's long-term strategies are evolving within the framework of a number of global trends. The first of these is that the tire industry and, indeed, the rubber industry are mature industries. In international terms, this has meant that, with a relatively slowly growing market, firms compete largely on the basis of costs of production, which are to a certain extent influenced by economies of scale. Thus there have been numerous mergers and takeovers in the industry, as witnessed by Taurus's moving from being the world's thirty-second largest tire producer in 1989 to twenty-first in 1990 as firms with larger production merged. Taurus has been approached regarding takeover possibilities but so far has shown no interest, perhaps in part due to the uncertainties of its future under privatization.

A second long-term trend is the growing predominance of radial tires in the truck market, and, although bias-ply tires continue to dominate the market for agricultural vehicles, Taurus is producing radial tires for both markets.

The firm has developed plans to acquire new technology, some through joint ventures with Western firms, in order both to strengthen its abilities in traditional areas and to facilitate some measure of diversification into more dynamic activities, especially in nontire activities. A number of joint ventures is in place.

Although the firm saw a 20-percent decline in demand over the past two years as the result of the collapse of CMEA trade, it benefited from strategic decisions made in the late 1970s to place greater reliance on exports to Western markets. This, plus the depreciation of the forint *vis-à-vis* Western currencies, has led to generally growing forint revenues, although the ongoing inflation in Hungary makes financial data of limited value.

Corporate Operations

Taurus, while nominally government owned, has been operating under the control of its corporate council. Thus, state ownership has not been manifested in the imposition of microeconomic goals. The prices of the firm's output have been largely decontrolled, and it is free to set its business strategy and to make Western investments that it considers desirable. After the respondents made these claims, it became evident that some qualifications to this picture of sweeping autonomy were necessary along the following lines:

—there were rather specific price equalization taxes and taxes on exports to the CMEA;

—there were general complaints that the government saddles firms with social and political objectives, yet expects them to be profitable. While respondents acknowledged that the government's mandates on fringe benefits were acceptable, they argued that they would wish to shut down some product lines and eliminate some 800–900 workers, but this was not economical due to wage and tax regulations;

—there seem to be a number of formal and informal ratios of performance variables to which the firm is expected to adhere.

Financial Performance

The principal problem the firm faces is the result of the shortage of credit and the resulting expansion of interenterprise debt. Under the prereform system, the firm needed much less working capital as domestic deliveries were paid in eight days and CMEA exports were credited when they crossed the Hungarian border. The move toward convertible-currency markets, where terms are 30 to 90 days, is only partly responsible for the payment delays the firm is experiencing. About three-fourths of the firm's domestic receivables are 30–60 days overdue. The firm charges interest on these overdue payments, but this is seen as neither preventing the erosion of these assets by inflation nor expediting payment. Indeed, in many cases the interest on overdue invoices seems not to be paid. The obvious response for Taurus is to delay its own payments to suppliers to the maximum extent possible. It has generally exhausted its possibilities for raising short-term capital. Thus the company's short-term assets and liabilities have grown much more rapidly than the other items on its balance sheet.

The firm foresees the greatest dangers facing it as coming from the financial sphere. If the outstanding debts of enterprises to each other cannot be regularized and turned into bank debt or discounted, then the firm may become saddled with the bad debts of its customers or experience difficulties from a shortage of working capital. A second incipient source of difficulty is government pressure, both at the national and at the local level, to preserve employment at the expense of profits.

Summary

Because the firm is oriented toward the West, it has suffered less than many other firms from the collapse of the CMEA, although the effects of the CMEA shock have not been negligible. Moreover, the strong hard-currency earnings of the firm give it a measure of independence. Nevertheless, it has not been able to escape the effects of the Hungarian liquidity crunch. Also evident is the fact that the firm's strategic planning is somewhat behind that of Western tire makers, in part because of the firm's uncertainties regarding future privatization. Taurus has undertaken some restructuring, aided in part by the advice of Western consultants retained under a World Bank program, but it appears that the execution of this restructuring program is hampered both by the credit crunch that faces the firm and, perhaps more importantly, by the perception of explicit and implicit limits on the amount of restructuring that would be tolerated by the government and by society. The possibility of Taurus's abandonment of certain product lines raises the specter of increased imports, a consequent deterioration of the balance of payments and increased unemployment with its macroeconomic and regional implications. While some of these concerns would also impinge on the strategic decisions of a firm in a West European country, they would not play as important a role as they do in Hungary.

4.2 Müszertechnika

Company Background

Müszertechnika is a privately owned firm with over 400 employees and a 1990 turnover of about HUF 25 billion. It has subsidiaries abroad—in Switzerland, the United States, Taiwan, the Federal Republic of Germany, and Czechoslovakia—as well as in Hungary. The firm began as a cooperative in 1981 and quickly branched out from the manufacture of electrical instruments to the assembly of IBM-compatible computers and later to other areas of electronics. It also has offices for computer service and maintenance, for training computer users and operators, and for software development.

Markets

A. Current Market Situation

IBM-compatible personal computers (PCs) account for the largest share of the firm's business, and Müszertechnika is a major factor on the Hungarian market. Company executives believe that imports, primarily from the West, account for about 50 percent of domestic sales, while Müszertechnika accounts for 20–30 percent of domestic sales, or 40–60 percent of domestically produced sales. There are over 100 computer manufacturers in Hungary, although only 4 or 5 are large by industry standards. Currently, PCs account for about 70 percent of turnover, and 30 percent of turnover is exported.

The company is also engaged in the production of large-scale display boards for stadium, air- and rail-terminal, etc., use; asynchronous motor controllers; power distribution systems (with the cooperation of Brown-Boveri); and telecommunications equipment. The firm's venture into telecommunications equipment is also a partnership, with Ericsson, and was established to help that firm bid successfully to supply a switching center for the Hungarian telecommunications system. Some of these products are exported to the West. The firm does not export its PCs to the West, but it does export components and subsystems, such as disk-drive controllers and software, to German-speaking countries. The Soviet Union was the main market for the firm's computers. While the traditional form of trade with the USSR has virtually disappeared, Müszertechnika has continued to prosper in the Soviet market for two reasons. One is a willingness and ability to find customers and to develop a special relationship with each one. Second is the fact that Müszertechnika has a joint venture with a steel mill in Kazakhstan. Thus, even though Soviet firms now lack foreign exchange and are prohibited from engaging in barter trade (although a number of

Hungarian respondents indicated that "informal" barter trade with the USSR was in fact taking place, generally with the active or tacit cooperation of republic or municipal authorities in the USSR), the joint-venture arrangement permits the two partners to engage in a profitable form of barter trade.

Müszertechnika ships personal computers to its partner in the USSR; given the high price of PCs there, the sale of these computers to Soviet buyers is very profitable for the Soviet partner. This partner pays for the computers by trading steel for them. Then Müszertechnika undertakes to sell the steel in Western Europe (e.g., in Italy, Germany, etc.) and in the Far East. The Hungarian firm incurs considerable expenses in the disposal of the steel, using its personnel to oversee the shipment of the steel in the USSR, storing it in Hungary, and employing its agents to sell it in hard-currency markets. These costs come to about 50 percent of the value of the steel received from the Soviet partner. Nevertheless, this business is enormously profitable, and company officials appear to have little inclination to move out of this market prematurely.

B. Recent Market Trends and Market Strategies

Despite the current profitability of computer sales to the USSR, the firm recognizes that this market, or at least its present level of profitability, will not continue in the future. They cited both the possibility of political and economic instability in the USSR bringing a halt to their sales there and the likelihood that Soviet producers would eventually begin to assemble PCs from imported components in much the same way that Müszertechnika did. In addition to the eventual erosion of the Soviet market, competition, both foreign and domestic, has been driving down the price of computers in Hungary. Thus, the company is beginning to diversify away from computers; they currently account for 70 percent of sales, but their share will be only 50 percent within two years.

Emphasis will be placed instead on large display boards, the telecommunications venture with Ericsson, power transmission (with Brown-Boveri), some consumer electronics, computers for banks (with a Brazilian partner), and other possibilities. To some extent these are based on the firm's general expertise in electronics, and to some extent they are driven by market opportunities (for example, the partnership with Ericsson). Nevertheless, these diversification efforts are all dependent on finding an appropriate Western partner who can provide the technology and components as well as market the product in the West. Thus, Müszertechnika provides its strength on the Hungarian market, its skill and competitive costs in assembly operations, and its know-how in electronics. As such, the firm is dependent on its Western partners for the success of its diversification efforts.

Corporate Operations

Müszertechnika is 100 percent privately owned, with 125 shareholders, all of whom are natural persons and all of whom are affiliated with the company. Because it is not a public company, the shares are not yet traded. The firm wishes to make a private placement of shares for USD 10–15 million and then, within 12 months or so, to go public either through a domestic offering followed by a foreign one or directly on the Vienna Stock Exchange. There is also a possibility that the firm's foreign partners will choose to acquire some of its shares.

Given the ownership structure of the firm, management is entirely autonomous; there is no workers' council, and the firm's workers are not unionized. More than 150 of Müszertechnika's workers have university degrees, and the average wage is HUF 23,000 per month (versus the average industrial wage of HUF 10,000–15,000 per month). Labor costs are augmented by about 43 percent to cover insurance, wage taxes, and other fringes. R&D expenses are about 5–10 percent of revenues.

Financial Performance

Müszertechnika is profitable and will pay its first dividend in the spring of 1991; on the advice of its bankers, it is continuing to reinvest the bulk of its profits. Because of the relatively liquid position of the company, it was able to pay those accounts payable that it wished to pay; presumably in cases where it was seen as possible and advantageous to delay payment, this may have been done. The firm has experienced delays in payments from state-owned Hungarian firms. Its usual payment terms are 15 days, but actual payments are running about 30 days beyond that, and to protect its financial position, the firm has borrowed to cover accounts receivable at a nominal rate of 32 percent, which is most likely a negative real rate.

Conclusions

Because the firm is a private one, its finances are stronger than those of many state-owned firms interviewed, and this has helped the firm in the current circumstances. The firm has not suffered from the collapse of trade with the USSR, although its situation is unique. In general, the profitability of its computer operations depends on existing barriers and market imperfections in the former CMEA countries and on the availability of computer components. The firm's leadership recognizes that long-run viability will depend on the ability to develop products whose profitability depends more on genuine competitiveness on world markets and less on exploiting trade barriers and market imperfections. In general, the way toward this end is being sought through joint ventures with Western firms. Müszertechnika has considerable room for maneuver in developing its business strategies, but such high dependence on foreign partners may impose new types of constraints on future decisions.

4.3 Szim

Company Background

Szim is a state-owned enterprise in the machine-tool industry. The firm was established in 1963 when the government combined a number of machine-tool enterprises into one large multiplant concern. This arrangement proved satisfactory for the 1960s. In the mid-1970s, the firm borrowed money at the behest of the state, say company officials, to update its technology. Repaying these loans proved difficult in the latter part of the decade due to the downturn of the Hungarian economy and due to greater fiscal stringency.

The firm's difficulties led to a change in the management and the infusion of HUF 1.2 billion in the form of a loan to increase working capital and improve the firm's technology. The resulting restructuring reduced the labor force from 6,300 to 4,500, resulted in the sale of four factories, and changed the firm's output profile from simple to computer–numerically controlled (CNC) machine tools that have a higher unit value but are less material intensive. As a result, the consumption of steel castings fell from 13,000 tons per year to 2,300. Such a restructuring was painful and politically controversial, especially over the issues of redundant workers and factory closings. Nevertheless, the restructuring had the desired results in the sense that profits increased from HUF 56 million in 1980 to HUF 700 million in 1987. These profits appear to have been posted before the repayment of the loans, since the company's officials cited loan repayments as the reason why Szim failed to upgrade its production facilities in the 1980s.

Changes in the tax system and the fiscal and monetary policies of the late 1980s led to a further reorganization of the firm. Individual establishments were set up as independent firms, wholly owned by the central administration, which was recast in the form of a holding company. The latter assumed all the liabilities of the former Szim, which it hoped to service and eventually pay off with the profits of the eleven subsidiaries. The subsidiaries, being thus "cleaned up" from a financial standpoint, were able to appear as better joint-venture partners for Western firms. The number of employees in the subsidiary firms is 3,500–3,700, and turnover in 1990 was expected to be HUF 4–4.5 billion, reflecting the ongoing downsizing of the firm.

Markets

A. Current Market Situation

In the 1980s, between two-thirds and three-quarters of the firm's output was exported, with 30–40 percent of exports to hard-currency areas and the remainder to the CMEA market. Of CMEA sales, the Soviet Union accounted for 40 percent in 1990. Moreover, Szim's sales of pneumatic brake systems for trucks and buses, some 30 percent of turnover, were very dependent on the requirements of the Ikarus bus factory, whose sales to the USSR also collapsed in 1991.

Recent Market Trends

Szim anticipates no shipments to the USSR in 1991 because, although there is demand for Szim's products, Soviet firms have no hard currency and no intergovernmental trade agreement exists between Hungary and the USSR to provide financing. This collapse of Soviet demand, coupled with declines in sales to the rest of the CMEA and reduced investment within Hungary, leads Szim's management to anticipate a 40-percent decline in production in 1991.

Market Strategies

Szim is following a dual-track strategy. One track consists of efforts to strengthen marketing in the former CMEA countries. Szim's trading company is building up its sales organization in Romania, Czechoslovakia, and the USSR in the hope that the second half of 1991 and 1992 will see a recovery of trade with these countries. The hope is that such a revival of trade, possibly on the basis of *ad hoc* barter arrangements, would put Szim in a good competitive position if it can put out products that embody modern technology and that are competitive with Western products. Szim has also altered its product mix, moving from machine tools to equipment, such as a sausage-filling machine, that is likely to be in greater demand in the USSR.

The second track is to seek new markets in the West. This is being done in part through joint ventures and cooperation with Western firms that previously supplied technology to Szim. For example, the Szim subsidiary that previously produced pneumatic brake systems for Ikarus obtained technical and marketing assistance through a joint venture with the German firm Knorr Bremse, which had supplied the bus brake technology, so as to switch production to brake systems for trains. Similar efforts are being made in the machine-tool segment of Szim's business, sometimes on the basis of prior relations with Western firms, in other cases on the basis of new relationships. Given its excess capacity, Szim can offer Western firms the possibility of creating new capacities staffed by qualified and relatively inexpensive workers much more rapidly than could be achieved by building new facilities in Western Europe. An example of this type of strategy was a joint venture with the West German firm Maho. A complete production line for Maho machine tools was installed in Szim's Budapest factory from which the previous production equipment had all been removed and in a new building that Szim had constructed. The output will carry the Maho trademark and will represent an important source of hard-currency sales for Szim. Hungarian workers will be trained both in Germany and in Hungary. Szim's other operating companies are all being actively encouraged to develop similar partnerships, and several were reported to be in advanced stages of negotiation with Western partners. One success story was the subsidiary, Budapest Machine Tool Company, which produces about 300–350 CNC machines per year. In 1991 it has orders for over 200 machines from the West, including 104 from the United States and 70 from Germany.

Corporate Operations

Szim is a holding company, with production taking place in eleven subsidiaries and joint-stock companies and two limited-liability companies. Some of the production companies have foreign ownership, but the holding company has no outside owners. This lack of outside ownership in the holding company is likely to continue for several reasons. First, given the diversity of Szim's activities, a foreigner having ownership interest in the holding company could be in a compromising position *vis-à-vis* a Western rival who had a joint venture with one of Szim's operating subsidiaries. In any case, since the financial position of the holding company is worse than that of the operating affiliates, there is little foreign interest in the holding company.

Each of the operating firms has a workers' council, and workers are also represented in the affiliates' supervisory committee along with representatives of the owners, banks, and foreign-trade organizations. On the other hand, the holding company has only 23 employees, and thus it is not required to elect a workers' council. Instead, all the holding company employees, presumably mainly managers of various sorts, take part in the General Assembly.

Management believes that there will be little direct privatization of Szim, principally because the machine-tool sector is likely to experience more difficult times and thus profit opportunities will be greater for investors in other sectors. The operating companies will hopefully attract foreign investors through joint-venture arrangements, although management does not expect all the operating subsidiaries to survive the next few years.

Financial Performance

Szim is clearly struggling through a difficult period. The holding company holds the debt of the operating subsidiaries and thus carries the burden of trying to manage this debt while allocating resources among the operating subsidiaries. In part this reflects the old Hungarian pattern of cross subsidization, with profitable units taxed to subsidize loss-making ones. Management admits that some affiliates have not been able to fulfill their financial obligations to the holding company, yet they have not been shut down. In some cases, this subsidization is justified on the basis of a subsidiary's prospects. For example, the

Budapest Machine Tool Co., mentioned above, suffered a fall in sales from HUF 1.6 billion in 1989 to HUF 1.2 million in 1990 and suffered a very large loss in the latter year because it incurred a series of cancellations of orders after it had purchased the materials needed to fulfill these orders. The holding company kept the subsidiary afloat because of its good prospects in Western markets.

Nevertheless, it is difficult to tell how much such cross subsidization reflects good future prospects and how much represents the difficulty of downsizing the firm in the face of a 40-percent decline in demand. Management admitted that further cuts in the labor force and perhaps liquidation of some of the subsidiaries would have to be undertaken. However, labor costs account for only 12–15 percent of production costs, and shedding workers is expensive. The firm must provide 1–3 months severance pay and often forgives employee debts to the firm incurred in the purchase of company housing. The total amount of such debts is a large sum of money.

Production has not been disrupted by difficulties in obtaining inputs of domestic origin or the foreign components that are critical for exports destined for the West. Indeed, company officials reported that Hungary's import liberalization had greatly reduced problems in obtaining foreign inputs.

Like other Hungarian firms, Szim has experienced increasing delays in payments from customers. In the past, CMEA exports based on intergovernmental agreements were paid in 10 days; on hard-currency exports, terms of payment were 6–12 months net. Now some subsidiaries have invoices outstanding that are 4–5 years old. As the subsidiaries are experiencing delays in payments, they are also delaying their payments to the holding company. Thus the holding company, by being the last in line to get paid, is, in a sense, a source of credit to the subsidiaries.

Conclusions

The difficulties of the machine-tool sector appear to be long-term ones. The various administrative reorganizations and refinancings of the past reflect both the lack of competitiveness of the sector and the difficulty in downsizing the industry and concentrating its efforts in a narrower range of products. Past restructurings and infusions of capital never fully addressed these problems, and thus Szim now finds itself with accumulated debts from the past and a collapsed CMEA market. The strategy of cleaning up the finances of the operating companies in order to make them attractive joint-venture partners for Western firms is a reasonable one, so long as their debts to the holding company remain relatively "soft." However, this strategy does mean that the ultimate size and product mix of Szim will depend on which Western firms negotiate joint ventures with the operating companies. This lack of strategic control over Szim's future direction makes the holding company rather immaterial except as a repository of bad debt. However, without access to meaningful resources combined with the equally important right to close affiliates and shed labor as required, it is unclear precisely what more the holding company can do in a strategic sense. A key problem facing management is that there is a need for a physical restructuring and reorganization of the firm at the same time that management must deal with the repayment of old debts. The strategy of management appears to be to turn Szim into a profitable firm first and to worry about debt later. The financial environment in Hungary may be conducive to such a strategy, but there is a danger that by the time Szim becomes profitable on a day-to-day basis it will be so awash in debt that the company may never achieve viability and the holding company and its debts will have to be written off while some of the subsidiaries survive.

4.4 Gedeon Richter Chemical Works (GR)

Company Background

GR is the nationalized successor of one of Hungary's premier pharmaceutical firms, which was established in 1923. It is currently organized as a shareholding company, with the Hungarian Commercial Credit Bank holding 10 percent of the shares, a German partner 0.5 percent, and the state the remainder. The firm is in the midst of being privatized, and it was selected for early privatization because of its strong condition, the importance placed by Hungarian authorities on the future of the Hungarian pharmaceutical industry, which has a long and successful tradition, and the importance of international trade and technology transfer in the pharmaceutical industry.

Markets

Current Market Situation

GR had sales of HUF 17 billion in 1990. Products included ethical drugs (ethical drugs are those that are prescribed by physicians as opposed to so-called proprietary drugs, which are sold to the public without a doctor's prescription), such as steroids, peptides, antibacterial agents, and contraceptives, as well as cosmetics, veterinary products, and agro-chemicals, the latter three categories accounting for 5 percent of sales. About 20 percent of GR's output is consumed within Hungary, and the remainder is exported. About one-half of exports, 40 percent of sales, go to the West and the remainder to the former CMEA countries, with the USSR accounting for about two-thirds of CMEA deliveries. Unlike other Hungarian firms, whose sales to the USSR had collapsed in 1991, there has not been such a great decline in GR's exports to the CMEA countries, although there have been payment delays on the Soviet side.

Recent Market Trends

A major change has occurred on the domestic market for GR's ethical drugs. All pharmaceuticals consumed in Hungary had been subsidized by the government. The government's objective was to keep prices low, so it failed to include any markup for R&D expenditures in the prices. This is a problem faced by pharmaceutical companies worldwide; R&D expenditures *in toto* are very high, in part because much R&D activity never comes up with a marketable drug, but governments wish to allow at most a markup only on successful drugs covering only that particular drug's development costs. In Hungary, the government was supposed to cover R&D costs through transfers of funds to the drug companies.

This system had a number of implications:

—the prices of pharmaceuticals in Hungary were very low, about one-half the cost of imports of comparable generic drugs;

—the government had considerable control over domestic producers' marketing strategies as it licensed all drug imports and allocated the production of various drugs among Hungarian pharmaceutical firms.

In 1989 the system was changed by placing health expenditures under the social security budget and separating that budget from general government expenditures. The social security budget lacks funds for financing the R&D expenditures of the pharmaceutical firms, yet the firms are not permitted to raise domestic sales to cover their R&D costs. Moreover, GR has had to improve the packaging of drugs and has faced rising input costs, so that with fixed output prices the profitability of domestic sales has fallen.

GR has made the decision to remain in the Soviet market. This partly reflects the sunk costs of having conducted clinical trials of its drugs in that country to get them approved and the fact that the Soviet Union continues to purchase drugs from GR. In 1990 sales to the USSR amounted to USD 250 million, and in 1991 the company expected sales of USD 200 million. Officials estimate that the firm has about 15 percent of the Soviet market for pharmaceuticals. Richter faces some difficulty in negotiating appropriate prices with the Soviet Foreign Trade Corporation (FTC) that imports pharmaceuticals, as the FTC's budget is fixed, and it thus wishes to pay low prices. Since 1990, payments for pharmaceutical exports to CMEA countries were settled in hard currencies, partly under the impetus of a Hungarian tax of 30 percent on ruble exports. GR reported that in 1990 hard-currency settlements worked well, but in 1991 there were payment delays, particularly in the case of the USSR. GR participates in Medimpex, a trading company that handles exports to the Soviet Union for the Hungarian pharmaceutical industry and has already established sales offices in several of the Soviet republics.

Market Strategies

The company hopes to maintain its strong position in the former CMEA market while expanding sales to the West. Because the pharmaceutical industry is highly internationalized, with all firms seeking the widest distribution of their drugs in order better to amortize R&D expenditures, it is important for GR to find a Western partner as part of the privatization process who will enable GR to reach Western markets effectively. GR also wishes to strengthen its product line, and it has some promising drugs under development, although lack of adequate financing is hampering its efforts.

Corporate Operations

A large part of the firm's efforts are directed toward its privatization in the so-called first wave of privatization of Hungary's blue-chip companies. The firm will be reconstituted as a joint-stock company, and a Western partner will be sought who will purchase about one-half of the shares. This will allow GR to expand its facilities and increase its working capital. Subsequently there will be an offering of shares in Hungary.

Richter has good contacts with Western pharmaceutical firms, both through purchases and sales of pharmaceutical intermediates on the world market and through purchases and sales of technology and licenses. It is also seeking advice from Western banks about its choice of a partner. As yet neither the change in corporate structure nor the search for a partner has had a significant impact on day-to-day operations.

An important part of maintaining competitiveness in the pharmaceutical field is the discovery of new drugs and bringing them to market. The latter is both time consuming, sometimes taking as long as 10–12 years, and expensive, up to USD 200 million per drug. When a drug is identified as having potentially useful medical properties, a lengthy series of tests of efficacy, toxicity, and side effects must be conducted, first on animals and then on human subjects. Before a drug can be marketed, it must be approved by national authorities, which can only be done on the basis of clinical trials that often must be replicated in each country where approval is sought. Richter has six new products under development, and finding sufficient funds to bring these drugs to market is a serious problem for management.

Financial Performance

The firm is profitable, although profits have been squeezed by developments on the domestic market and by difficulties on the CMEA market as well. The firm has experienced delays in payment by the USSR as well as delays by Hungarian banks in clearing the payments. Hungarian government payments for drugs have been subject to greater delays than in the past. GR is consequently borrowing to maintain its liquidity and is able to pay its suppliers on a current basis. Nevertheless, the accumulation of receivables and the need to acquire short-term debt is of considerable concern to management and to the firm's Western advisers. A large accumulation of questionable assets and short-term debts will make the firm less attractive to potential Western partners.

Conclusions

The fact that GR is a source of pharmaceuticals that would otherwise have to be obtained in the West at higher prices has kept its trade with the Soviet Union from declining as much as that of other Hungarian firms. Also important is the fact that the import of pharmaceuticals in the USSR continues to be centralized in one trading company and purchases are financed from central funds. How this will evolve in the future will be a key issue for GR.

A second important question is one of choosing a Western partner. Management believes that a major pharmaceutical firm from the United States or Western Europe is likely to see GR primarily as an entryway to the Soviet and East European markets. Such a firm would also offer a strong retail network in Western Europe and North America, although it is not evident to what extent the partner would wish to use GR as a major source for those markets. On the other hand, a Japanese partner would be more likely to view GR as a potential entryway not only to the former CMEA market but also, and more importantly, to the EC market. In the long run, this might yield greater exports for the Hungarian firm, but in the short run it may be less attractive since such a strategy would require the creation of a new marketing network in Western Europe. In the short run, the firm faces liquidity problems, although these are not as life threatening as those faced by other Hungarian firms.

4.5 Budaprint

Company Background

Budaprint is a state-owned holding company whose subsidiaries produce HUF 12 billion of textile products and employ 8,500 people. Its principal products are cotton textiles, which account for 20–30 percent of turnover but whose share in output is declining, and printed fabrics. The firm had its beginning in 1963 when eight textile firms employing some 25,000 workers were merged into one unit. The company's organization was changed again in 1989, when a holding company and seven subsidiaries organized as shareholding or limited-liability companies were formed.

Markets

Current Market Situation

Budaprint used to export about 60 percent of its production, with exports split about evenly between the CMEA market and the West. Export transactions were handled by Budaprint's own Foreign Trade

Corporation. The remaining 40 percent of production was destined for the domestic market, where it was distributed by an affiliate through shops and catalogs. Budaprint's share of the domestic market has declined from 35 percent in 1988 to 20 percent in 1990, largely due to competition from imports.

Recent Market Trends

Budaprint suffered a sharp decline in demand on all its markets in 1990. Domestic demand declined by 15 percent in nominal terms in 1991. CMEA and Western sales also contracted, and the Hungarian textile industry saw its production fall by 20 percent in the course of the year. Moreover, textile prices on the domestic market have fallen. Under the old pricing system, which existed through 1988, Budaprint's domestic prices were supposed to reflect world market prices, but with textile imports severely restricted by the government, the company was able to set prices to provide a 3–5 percent profit margin. The import liberalization of 1990 made the need to price to the world market real, and Budaprint had to adjust prices to meet foreign competition on the domestic market.

Market Strategies

The company is responding to a worsening market situation largely by reducing output in an effort to avert bankruptcy.

Corporate Operations

As the company is now unprofitable and its losses are being covered by the government, management must decide what to do. One possibility is privatization, where the firm would be sold to investors and the proceeds used to pay off some of the government's contributions that are now used to cover operating losses. This possibility is, however, outside the scope of competence of Budaprint; such a decision to privatize would have to be made by the government. The other possibility would be for Budaprint to declare bankruptcy under the terms set out in Hungary's bankruptcy law. This law, however, is almost never invoked, either by loss-making firms or by their creditors, and its use is not contemplated by Budaprint's managers.

Thus the company continues to respond to market developments by reducing production and employment. Employment fell by 17 percent in 1989–90, and further cuts are anticipated. Moreover, average real wages have fallen because nominal wage growth has not kept up with inflation. Thus in 1989 the average wage was HUF 100,000 per year, and in 1990 it was HUF 120,000 per year, while the official estimate of inflation was 28 percent. Finally, the shedding of labor has been matched by a failure to renew the capital stock. In particular, the yarn-making and weaving operations are quite outdated in all subsidiaries, although there are some other operations that are quite modern. The average age of machinery in the subsidiaries is about 10 years.

In addition to a decline in demand, the firm has faced difficulties in the import of cotton, its primary raw material. This used to be imported mainly from the USSR, but these supplies have been disrupted. In 1989, the firm had to supplement Soviet supplies with purchases in Greece, and company officials were uncertain how much, if any, cotton they could expect for 1991 from the USSR. This has had a financial and strategic impact on Budaprint, since Soviet cotton was cheaper than that available on world markets by some 35 percent, but it is also of lower quality. Thus the need to substitute Western cotton imposes an additional financial strain on the firm. Moreover, because foreign cotton is of higher quality, Budaprint is attempting to produce fabrics of higher quality for more fashionable uses.

Financial Performance

The profitability of the firm has been declining for some time, and in 1990 it lost HUF 120 million. The firm owes debts both to banks and to suppliers of gas and electricity, and it is unable to pay some of its tax liabilities. Net debt is estimated to be 40–45 percent of group assets. The share of interenterprise debt is rising and the share of bank credit declining because banks are reducing their loans. The firm thus faces severe liquidity problems, and management must husband resources to maintain sufficient liquidity to purchase imported inputs, since payments to foreign suppliers, unlike those to domestic ones, cannot be delayed.

Conclusions

Budaprint's slow and gradual slide into insolvency has left it with a weak financial structure, few competitive advantages, and no strategic plan for revising its fortunes. It is likely that the Hungarian government tolerated Budaprint's existence on the basis of the fact that it was a net earner of both dollars and rubles, with normal year exports of USD 26 million and 32 million rubles. With firms now expected to earn a profit and both Western and former CMEA sales falling, there is little to justify the subsidy costs of these shrinking trade surpluses. Thus management views 1991 as the crisis year. Demand for its output is down in both domestic and foreign markets, debts are mounting, none of the affiliates are financially viable, and management appears unable to cope with the situation. Respondents also complained that the government had no policy toward the industry, although one might argue, albeit somewhat unkindly, that "having a policy" is likely to mean, at least to people in the industry, an injection of resources and that the government's neglect was, in fact, a policy designed to eliminate loss-making firms in the textile sector.

4.6 Hungarian National Oil and Gas Trust (OKGT)

Company Background

The firm is involved in exploration, transportation, refining, and distribution of oil and gas in Hungary. The firm is being reorganized on the basis of a World Bank loan that was made in 1989 to help the company restructure so as to:

—update and strengthen management information systems;

—allow energy prices to reflect world market prices more accurately by removing subsidies;

—separate the production of oil and gas from the distribution network and convert the oil operation into a national oil company;

—allow foreigners to participate in exploration activities;

—raise needed new capital, including foreign capital, through privatization.

This reorganization was going on at the time the firm was first interviewed and was the main management issue facing the firm.

Corporate Operations

Prior to 1991, the company operated its activities in the production, distribution, and wholesaling of oil and natural gas on an integrated basis. There were 23 separate companies, but each was vertically integrated.

Moreover, OKGT had a monopoly over the retailing of gasoline, and the distribution of natural gas to households was organized in 5 firms, each with a monopoly in a particular region of Hungary, although distribution of natural gas in Budapest was not part of OKGT's activities. The firm was in the midst of implementing major organizational changes. It has a variety of affiliates in the following fields:

—exploration and transportation;

—gas supply, which will be decentralized;

—machine manufacture and construction, which will become an independent privatized firm;

—technical development, which will become an independent private firm;

—gas supply. The five regional distribution firms will become independent. On July 1, 1991, they became subject to the Ministry of Industry rather than to OKGT. They will become joint-stock companies through a process to be supervised by the Ministry of Industry and the State Property Agency. At first, the state will own 80 percent of the shares and local bodies 20 percent. In 1992, the firms will make a public offering of stock equal to 50 percent of the state's share. They will further expand private shareholding by means of an ESOP (Employee Stock Ownership Program). Foreign investors will be able to purchase up to 45 percent of the equity of these firms, and talks are under way with Western gas firms to develop such purchases.

OKGT officials indicated that this phase of the restructuring of the firm was being held up by the following problems:

—failure to set up the joint-stock companies;

—lack of laws for:

• permitting local bodies to become part owners of distribution companies;

• regulating licensing and concessions for public utilities;

• creating a system of regulatory agencies for private and profit-oriented public-utility companies.

There are 11 companies involved in the refining, marketing, and exploration activities of OKGT. These will be regrouped along one of the three following alternatives:

1. totally independent joint-stock companies with no integrating framework; this option is not favored by OKGT;

2. nine companies merged into two separate joint-stock companies, one for research, exploration, production, and transportation of gas, the

other for refining and marketing. OKGT officials believe this arrangement would be attractive to foreign investors;

3. nine companies merged into one joint-stock company with upstream and downstream activities separated into two divisions. This alternative appears to be favored by the World Bank.

OKGT believes that investment and foreign participation are most needed in refining and in reducing Hungary's dependence on Soviet deliveries of oil and gas. These have fallen, officials reported, forcing the company to seek substitutes on the spot market.

Conclusions

The reorganization of OKGT reflects the problems of dismantling an organizational structure that was consistent with a planned economy, i.e., vertical integration to minimize the need for planning of input and output flows, and of creating one that will be consistent with a market economy. This should permit a more rational evaluation of the value of various services and thus a better allocation of investment in the gas and oil sector. At the same time, it is hard to project how profitable the new units will be and whether they can mesh together smoothly in what is likely to be a chaotic period for the Hungarian energy sector.

Chapter 5

Firms Afloat and Firms Adrift
Case Studies, 1992

The firms described in the previous chapter were reinterviewed in the spring and summer of 1992. Because the background of each firm was described fully in the preceding chapter, the updates are relatively brief and focus on those areas that were viewed as key or strategic for each firm. It is worth noting that not all firms survived the year or more between interviews with unchanged legal form and enterprise structure. This close-up view of the disappearance or metamorphosis of Hungarian firms is both poignant and instructive for understanding the transformation process at a microlevel.

5.1 Taurus

The 1991 financial year ended with heavy losses for the firm. It made some profit before tax, but interest payments on short-term credits were much greater than this profit. The stock of short-term credit increased by 35 percent between 1990 and 1991, and most of this increment was used for interest payments. Sales receipts reached HUF 16 billion in 1991, which was HUF 2.2 billion less than in 1990. This decline was due to the shrinking of the firm's domestic market shares, since between 1990 and 1991 its convertible-currency exports actually increased from HUF 8.5 billion to HUF 8.6 billion, approximately USD 105 million.

Taurus has two main profiles. One is tire production, and this division has been a source of losses for several years; tire production was also a loss maker for most major multinational firms in 1990. Import liberalization was a nearly fatal blow to the firm because its profits originated from its quasi-monopolistic sales of imported tires on the domestic market during most of the 1980s.

The second main division is rubber products used in oil production. This division has suffered from payment problems on its traditional Soviet, and later CIS, market, although its products are in high demand there.

The number-one strategic task now faced by management is privatization. The enterprise ought to have been transformed into a corporation in March or April 1992, but the State Property Agency did not give its approval. The reason was the firm's huge debt, altogether around HUF 2.5 billion. The company avoided bankruptcy only through a deal with the Hungarian Credit Bank, which agreed to provide short-term financing to the firm. If it had not done so, Taurus would have been forced by the new Bankruptcy Law to declare bankruptcy after 90 days of nonpayment of its arrears. The bank's strategy toward Taurus now seems to take an active interest in its privatization. A possible solution that the bank would be apparently ready to negotiate is a debt–equity swap. This would mean a swap of the firm's long-term debts for its shares during transformation.

Although the only positive step definitely taken by the bank was its commitment to maintain current financing, this was enough for the SPA to give a green light to the transformation process. As the differences among the financial situations of the different plants of Taurus became more and more evident, the former holding-based transformation approach lost most of its support. The firm will transform itself into six independent joint-stock companies using the same brand name, and foreign investors are expected to participate separately in them.

The value of the net assets of the firm is estimated at around HUF 5 billion, which gives most of its successors relatively good prospects of privatization. The privatization process seems to be hampered by the fact that the tire division, or its successor firm, is considered by foreign investors as an uninteresting low-technology part of the worldwide overcapacity in tire production. It might well transpire, therefore, that the tire division, or the Budapest plant within it, cannot be privatized at all. The failure of negotiations with Michelin and Goodyear also points to this conclusion. Thus, the firm's inability to resolve all its strategic handicaps has left it with no alternative but partition, dismemberment, and bankruptcy for some plants.

5.2 Müszertechnika

The company is still considered one of the most successful national private firms in Hungary, although the Kontrax group also has had very favorable press coverage. Müszertechnika is by and large on the same development track as in early 1991. The major developments have been in the realm of mergers and acquisitions, although the firm itself has been less active than its principal shareholder and president-CEO, Mr. Gábor Széles, who owns 28 percent of its shares.

The firm itself has teamed up with two major multinational firms. One of them is IBM, with which Müszertechnika created a hardware- and software-making joint venture (JV) also interested in foreign trade. This joint venture is expected to be the number one player on the Hungarian and eventually also on the East European market for computer technology and equipment, but exact figures on its financial strength and technical size are not yet available.

The other strategic alliance was concluded with Ericsson in early 1990. This initially very small JV was created in order to help Müszertechnika enter the rapidly expanding Hungarian telecom equipment market. The joint venture was one of the winners of the 1990 switchboard tender, which guarantees a 35–65 percent share of the domestic market for telecommunications equipment between 1991 and 1996 for the JV. This made it possible for the JV to increase its employees from 2 in January 1990 to 180 in May 1992. Its annual sales are planned to reach HUF 1 billion in 1992.

The president-CEO of Müszertechnika, a firm with approximately HUF 9 billion in annual sales, made a very courageous step in 1991 when he acquired a qualified 10-percent equity stake in the Videoton group, with annual sales of HUF 12–15 billion. Although Videoton has been a holding-based group with a negative book value of assets due to its HUF 25 billion debt, most of its capacities represent a reasonably high technological standard. The acquisition of these capacities is probably the first step toward the creation of a Müszertechnika group of electronics firms.

Thus by retaining its financial viability, Müszertechnika has been able to follow its strategic and technological objectives relatively successfully.

5.3 Szim

The Hungarian machine-tools industry is near extinction due to its financial problems linked to the collapse of domestic demand and traditional export markets in CMEA countries. Szim as a group does not have serious chances of survival either.

Szim transformed itself into a holding-based industrial conglomerate in

1988. Therefore, it provided one of the examples of spontaneous privatization with the setting up of an empty-shell–type holding. Ten subsidiaries were created around the holding. Out of these subsidiaries, two joint ventures, Maho–Szim and Knorr-Bremse–Szim, proved successful, and their business prospects are really reassuring. Four other subsidiaries, however, are already under liquidation, and two or three more could join them shortly due to the new bankruptcy legislation.

The privatization of the group has been a very complicated process. The strategy of the management of the holding was focused on the creation of strong JVs. If all the assets of the group and the holding could have been transferred to these ventures, the holding would have liquidated itself. The success of this strategy strongly depended on a deal struck with the SPA. This deal was part of the group's privatization program, and it stipulated that half the state revenue from the sale of the group's assets could be used to prepare the different subsidiaries for privatization. This deal worked for one subsidiary or two, but it could not be taken for granted that the SPA would stick to the old deal after some candidates for privatization began to face the danger of liquidation. After liquidation, the complicated privatization problem of the subsidiaries would become a much simpler one of selling their assets. In any event, the thirty-year-old Szim story will come to an end soon, and this end will not be a happy one.

5.4 Gedeon Richter Chemical Works

Gedeon Richter had a successful year in 1991, with profits before tax up by 43 percent from their 1990 level, reaching HUF 1.14 billion. As the biggest Hungarian pharmaceutical firm, it is in an advantageous position for further privatization. Details are not known, but management is probably negotiating with a major Japanese investor. Management has been reluctant to talk about the current situation of the company. This confirms expectations that privatization will take place soon.

Gedeon Richter, a limited-share company, will increase its capital prior to privatization. Shareholders took a quite conservative approach at the general assembly, with 86 percent of the 1991 profit used for an increase of the reserve capital of the firm and only 14 percent paid out as dividends.

Some performance data are available for the company, but they cannot really be compared with the 1990 results due to the fact that Gedeon Richter underwent transformation and reorganization, with some privatization at the same time. For example, employment decreased from 6,119 to 5,941 between 1990 and 1991, while net sales increased from HUF 4.2 billion to HUF 16.1 billion and exports from HUF 3.0 billion to HUF 10.7 billion. The book value of assets also remained almost the same, HUF 17.2 billion in 1991 as compared to HUF 16.7 billion in 1990.

5.5 Budaprint

The firm has been operating since 1989 as a holding-based group. The holding is a typical empty shell employing only 23 persons. Its major source of revenue is leasing to its subsidiaries. The combined output of the subsidiaries is only 30 million square meters of cloth, one-fourth of mid-1980s production. This substantial shrinking of output has been mainly due to the collapse of exports to the Soviet market. While employment surpassed 23,000 in 1985, the group now has less than 10,000 employees and jobs are lost continuously. The reason for the ongoing crisis is undercapitalization, which leads to decreasing competitiveness on Western markets. Sales on the domestic market offer no solution because the decline in living standards in Hungary has sharply reduced the household consumption of textiles and clothing. Undercapitalization is further exacerbated by the indebtedness of most of the subsidiaries. An injection of capital was expected from privatization, but privatization did not take place in any of the five productive subsidiaries.

This was no surprise because these companies have neither high-value assets nor significant market shares to offer. Therefore, some subsidiaries looked for such new privatization techniques as debt–equity swaps with major creditor banks. Another option would be the transformation of real-estate leasing agreements between the holding and the subsidiaries into an increase of the equity stake of the holding in them. Although this option is also being negotiated, its implementation would not help resuscitate the productive activities of the subsidiaries. Some of them do not, in fact, rule out the possibility of partly becoming real-estate trading or leasing firms. Along with Szim, the case of Budaprint is another symptom of Hungarian deindustrialization.

5.6 Hungarian National Oil and Gas Trust (OKGT)

OKGT has been known under a new name in Hungary since October 1, 1991, the day of its legal transformation: MOL Rt, a corporation limited by shares. MOL Rt is the legal successor of OKGT, but it is a much smaller firm. It does not include some service firms and equipment manufacturers that formerly belonged to OKGT, although it has an equity stake in some of them, while it leases land and equipment to others. The privatization of these independent successors of OKGT is possible, but MOL Rt itself belongs to the group of strategic firms in which the state will keep majority ownership.

The transformed structure of MOL Rt consists of two major divisions: (1) prospecting and production (extraction); and (2) oil and gas processing and sales. These divisions are profit centers, and the top management of MOL Rt retained only strategic decision-making functions for itself. The second profit center is at least by one order of magnitude bigger than the first one. It includes the four big Hungarian refinery plants as well as ÅFOR, the retail arm of MOL Rt, which operates gas stations across the country.

The economic prospects of MOL Rt are somewhat uncertain due to the half-hearted deregulation of the oil and gas sector. The firm will have to enter an almost completely open competition in domestic prospecting and extraction due to the new concession legislation, but it operates in a regulated domestic market environment as a seller of oil and gas products. Its profits reached HUF 35 billion in 1991, HUF 6 billion less than in 1990. This profit is just at the minimally acceptable level for this very capital-intensive company, which has also been hit by the severe taxation on the use of mineral resources and by antitrust regulations. The latter do not allow for automatic consumer price increases of oil and gas products in case the firm's increasing costs make them necessary.

The taxation of the use of mineral resources takes an especially drastic form in the Hungarian oil and gas industry. MOL Rt has to transfer 37.5 percent of the current world-market-price–based equivalent of the oil and gas extracted to the state budget immediately, long before these are refined, processed, and sold. This leads to significant interest losses for the firm due to the high nominal interest rates in Hungary, which have not been reflected in oil and gas price increases. MOL Rt transferred HUF 146 billion (USD 1.8 billion) to the budget in 1991, 39 percent of the sales revenues of the company.

5.7 Conclusions from the Case Study Updates

The updates give a quite reliable impression of the 1992 situation of Hungarian industry as a whole. Basically three groups of firms can be observed in the sample, and the same three groups are distinguishable in Hungarian industry altogether. Group 1 is that of firms in a promising situation and with good prospects for expansion. These are, in general, new private companies or, in a few cases, big state firms in monopolistic positions. In spite of its problems, MOL Rt belongs to the latter type of firms, whereas Müszertechnika is a strongly expanding private company with good chances of becoming an industrial giant, in Hungarian circumstances, of course. Richter is a rather special case, since it belongs to the small number of state, or quasi-state, firms performing well even according to international standards. This is true, by the way, for most of Hungarian pharmaceutical firms.

Group 2 is that of drifting firms. This is the behavioral pattern among Hungarian firms that deserves the most attention in research for at least two reasons.

First, this type of behavior is quite new in the literature, which has known only two fundamental types of enterprise behavior: produce or perish. This distinction supposes that any firm unable to increase its assets or to respond to the expectations of its owners in any other way has to face bankruptcy or liquidation in a market economy. There are, of course, well-known cases in market economies, e.g., Austrian, German, or French state firms such as VOEST, the Deutsche Bundesbahn, or Bull, that have been permanent loss makers during recent years without any real danger of liquidation. But these firms satisfy some special, albeit maybe only political, needs of their owners, i.e., their governments, while many drifting firms in Hungary are not kept alive by the government. They survive only due to their managers' insistence on grasping even the slightest chance of keeping the company alive.

Many Hungarian firms, mostly state or recently privatized ones, are living off their assets but do not face immediate liquidation. The interest of their owner might be to liquidate them, but no one expresses this interest clearly enough. The managers of these firms play for time, aware of the fact that many Hungarian firms such as theirs are in a comparable situation, and a wave of liquidations would cause an earthquake-like shock for the whole economy.

The bankruptcy legislation in force from January 1, 1992, and applied from April 8 has increased the monthly average number of bankruptcies from approximately 240 to approximately 1,000, and it is predicted that half of these will end with liquidation. But there are many cases where agreements on debt settlement are reached between creditors and debtors because a really strict application of this law would result in the loss of most clients for banks and firms providing suppliers' credits on the domestic market. So far only about 7 percent of Hungarian firms have been liquidated even on the basis of this drastic bankruptcy law. This law is widely criticized for its one-sided legal structure, namely, that it provides protection only to the creditor but does not really help resolve the debtor's problems. For example, it makes bankruptcy unavoidable even for a firm that is a net creditor but is unable to repay just one of its debts due to liquidity problems originating from the irredeemability of its assets.

Second, drifting firms have been able to survive, and, due to the dwindling of the assets of most of them, they can be considered as increasingly interesting targets for investors. There is normally a point of inflexion in the process of the shrinking of their assets. This point of inflexion means the minimum of the book value of the assets of the company until a short time before liquidation is started. It often happens that the book value, or the sales price of the firm, increases somewhat immediately before liquidation, when owners and managers realize that privatization is no longer possible. In this case they are interested in demonstrating relatively high values of the assets of the firm in order to reach better debt settlements or debt–equity swaps.

Examples of the drifting type of firm, unable to grow but successfully avoiding liquidation, can be found in our sample, too. Taurus and Budaprint are such cases, albeit they are different with respect to the distance they have drifted away from a healthy financial and market situation. Neither of the two firms, or, more accurately, holding-based industrial conglomerates, will be able to survive as a whole, but Taurus seems to have a string of viable subsidiaries, while the drifting of Budaprint might well end in its becoming part of the third group of Hungarian industrial firms.

The third group is that of companies bound to disappear from the Hungarian economic scene unless they are rescued by the government. The Ministry of Industry and Trade has proposed a government rescue action for a dozen big state firms that are in a difficult financial situation but considered competitive if they get an appropriate injection of working capital. Their privatization is out of the question, in most cases because the combined value of their assets and liabilities is already negative.

Holding-based conglomerates are a special subset of the third group. In their case, most fixed capital usually belongs to the holding, frequently an empty shell, but the holding is responsible for the repayment of most of the debt of the former monolithic state firm. Managers of such holdings might find a way to rescue at least part of the productive subsidiaries of the holding. The solution normally consists either in the transfer of the legally transferable fixed assets from the holding to the subsidiaries while the holding remains the main debtor, or in debt–equity swaps in which creditors might obtain the holding's shares in part of the subsidiaries in exchange for credits.

Therefore the third group is far from being homogeneous, and it cannot be concluded that it will disappear as a whole. Parts of it might survive, but only as small or medium-sized enterprises with no significant debt load and a much narrower market niche than the original big state firm. This is the case of Szim, which, as the legal successor of the former monolithic state firm, i.e., the holding, is under liquidation, but at least two of its subsidiaries face a promising future. They belong to the first group of Hungarian industrial firms, and it might be interesting to mention that there are very few drifting firms in the environment of disappearing holdings. Options are clear for most subsidiaries of these after the disappearance of the holding: either long-term survival or liquidation together with or not much later than that of the holding.

Enterprise Behavior and Industrial Policy

Normally, drifting cannot be a long-term strategy, but its large-scale presence as a behavioral pattern among Hungarian industrial firms is a telling proof of the current transitional situation of the Hungarian economy. We estimate that around 60 percent of Hungarian industrial firms are now drifting to some extent, 15–20 percent are in serious danger of liquidation, whereas the rest, at least 20 percent, can make long-term plans.

The future of Hungarian industry, even the short-term one, largely depends on where the drifters will move. If most of them disappear in one year or two, this would mean a considerable deindustrialization process for Hungary. If most of them survive, there would be no significant structural change in Hungarian industry. A compromise scenario seems the most likely, in which 30–50 percent of the drifting enterprises cannot be long-term survivors. This would already mean a sizable structural cleanup process in Hungarian industry.

No precise forecast can be given of the direction of this far-reaching structural change, but its dimensions can be assessed to some extent. First of all, it will not simply mean macrostructural change with structural shifts only among industries. It will also have a regional and an enterprise dimension. The interaction of the three dimensions means that the reaction of each enterprise to this transformation of industry will largely depend not only on the change of the macrostructural role of the industry it belongs to. It will also be strongly influenced by the development of the region where the firm is located and the adjustment prospects of other firms with comparable types of ownership, size, market pattern, etc. Macrostructural change will have an increasingly average character, with fewer direct implications for the transformation of an industry or the firms that are part of it. Enterprise behavior and reaction to the crisis will therefore be conditional upon the development of the given industry and region and upon the type of enterprise.

It is likely, for example, that the clothing industry as such will not stop shrinking during the years 1992–93 or beyond, but there seem to be good prospects for small, newly created, i.e., not arising from privatization, and debt-free private firms in this industry. These would prosper either by subcontracting or by selling on nearby, demand–pull type foreign markets such as Ukraine or Romania. Eventually good export chances on these markets or widespread subcontracting for German, Italian, or Austrian firms means that clothing firms located in the western or the southeastern regions of the country will be much more promising than the average of the industry.

Such patterns of Hungarian industrial development will be recognized by industrial policy quite soon, and this policy will lose its unilateral macrostructure-oriented character. In recent months the Ministry of Industry and Trade has expressed more and more frequently its interest in stopping the deindustrialization process. Now it is ready to take an active part in enterprise crisis management for twelve big state firms facing bankruptcy and eventual liquidation due to external market factors beyond their control. It can also be expected that the ministry will play a more active role in regional crisis management because it has turned out, for example in the case of the DIMAG

Steel Works in Miskolc, that the government's hands-off approach has been unable to resolve major regional crisis situations without imposing a substantial additional burden on the state budget. Therefore, preventive regional crisis management, together with the restructuring of potentially privatizable state firms, will have to be incorporated into industrial policy. The financial basis of such a policy can be created from part of current privatization revenues. The use of these revenues is now limited by law to the repayment of the state debt, but it is clear that an eventual slowdown of the privatization process will threaten a deepening of the budget crisis, and this could be prevented only through state expenditures on preparing firms for privatization.

Finally, a serious methodological problem hampering the correct assessment of enterprise behavioral patterns has to be mentioned. Enterprises with clear nonstate ownership patterns are increasingly reluctant to be interviewed by researchers because they are afraid of data leakages that could be used by:

—pressure groups wishing to attack the management for political reasons;

—creditors eager to get a correct picture of the financial situation of the firm;

—competitors interested in hostile takeovers.

Their fears are partly justified by the fact that the legal framework for the protection of confidential business information is still missing. If the so-called Data Protection Act is adopted by parliament, managers will probably be easier to approach for information, but this law does not yet even figure on the agenda of the parliament.

Bibliography

This list is given in a slightly unconventional manner. The major part of the literature used exists only in Hungarian, therefore most titles are given only in English translation. These translations come from the English summaries of the articles to be found in nearly all of the economics periodicals appearing in Hungary. The reader will be able to find the original article on the basis of the name of the author and the usual bibliographical data. The omission of some Hungarian titles is thought to make the list more manageable. Where this happens, the reference is marked (H).

Antal, L. 1985. *Our Economic Management and Financial Mechanism on the Way to Reforms*. Budapest: KJK (H).

———. 1988. "Stabilization and Reform (Theses)." *Külgazdaság*, nos. 2–3: 246–54 (H).

Antal, L., and Surányi, Gy. 1987. "The Fore-History of the Banking System's Transformation." *Külgazdaság*, no. 1: 3–12 (H).

Antal, L., and Várhegyi, É. 1987. *Capital Flows in Hungary*. Budapest: KJK (H).

Balassa, B. 1986. "The 'New Growth Path' in Hungary." *Gazdaság*, no. 2: 24–46 (H).

Ballance, R., and Sinclair, S. 1983. *Collapse and Survival. Industrial Strategies in a Changing World*. London: Allen & Unwin.

Bauer, T. 1981. *Planned Economy, Investment, Cycles*. Budapest: KJK (H).

———. 1982. "The Second Economic Reform and Ownership Relations: Some Considerations for the Further Development of the New Economic Mechanism." *Mozgó Világ* 11: 17–42 (H); English version: *Eastern European Economics*, vol. 22, no. 2–3 (Spring–Summer 1984): 33–87.

———. 1987. "Instead of Cycles—Crisis?" *Közgazdasági Szemle*, no. 12: 1409–34 (H).

Berend, T.I. 1988. "The Turning Point of Hungarian Reform in the Seventies." *Valóság*, no. 1: 3–27 (H).

Bihari, M. 1987. "Reform and Democracy." *Medvetánc* (Special Volume), no. 2: 165–226 (H).

Bokros, L. 1987. "The Preconditions for the Evolving of Business Behavior in a Two-Level Banking System." *Külgazdaság*, no. 1: 21–32 (H).

Botos, B. 1991. "The Strategic Concept for Industry and Trade." *Ipari Szemle*, no. 1 (December): 2–7 (H).

Csikós-Nagy, B. 1988. "The Situation and Prospects of the Hungarian Economy." *Valóság*, no. 6 (H).

Erdős, T. 1991. "The Chances of an Economic Upturn." *Külgazdaság*, no. 12 (H).

FR (abbrev.). 1987. "Fordulat és Reform" (Turn and reform). *Medvetánc* (Special Volume), no. 2: 5–130 (H).

Friss, P. 1992. "Beruházás, állóeszköz-fenntartás" (Investment and the maintenance of fixed capital). *Gazdaság és Statisztika*, no. 2: 3–11.

Huszti, E. 1987. *At an Anti-inflationary Crossroads—Monetary Policy and Practice in Hungary*. Budapest: KJK (H).

Inotai, A. 1985. "How to Proceed? Trends of Manufacturing Exports." *Figyelő*, no. 36 (H).

JA (abbrev.) 1988. *Jelentések az Alagútból* (Reports from the tunnel). Budapest: Pénzügykutatási Rt. (Financial Research Corp.), June (H).

Kornai, J. 1986. "The Hungarian Reform Process: Visions, Hopes and Reality." *Journal of Economic Literature* 24: 1687–1737.

Köves, A., and Oblath, G. 1981. "Hungarian Foreign Trade in the Seventies." *Gazdaság*, no. 4 (H). In English: *Acta Oeconomica*, vol. 30, no. 1 (1983): 89–109.

Laki, M. 1992. "A vállalati magatartás változása és a gazdasági válság" (Changes in enterprise behavioral patterns and the economic crisis). Institute of Economics of the Hungarian Academy of Sciences Discussion Papers No. 5, Budapest.

Lengyel, L. 1987. "A Contribution to the History of 'Turn and Reform.' " *Medvetánc* (Special Volume), no. 12:131–63 (H).

Ligeti, S. 1987. "The Reorganization of the Banking System." *Külgazdaság*, no. 1: 13–20 (H).

Marer, P. 1988. *Economic Reforms and Performance in Hungary* (manuscript). Bloomington, IN: Indiana University Press, 1988.

Matolcsy, Gy. 1988. "From the State Enterprise to the Company." *Valóság*, no. 6: 66–79 (H).

Meisel, V.S., and Mohácsi, K. 1990. "Changes on the Hungarian Electronics Market." *Tervgazdasági Fórum*, no. 2 (H).

Meisel, S.; Mohácsi, K.; Salgó, I.; Szegvári, I.; and Török, A. 1988. "Foreign Economic Preconditions of Efficiency Orientedness." *Tervgazdasági Közlemények*, no. 2 (H).

Nagy, Z. 1988. "Regulatory System in the First Half of the 1980s" (mimeo). OT Tervgazdasági Intézet (Institute of the Economics of Planning of the National Planning Board), Budapest, April 1988 (H).

Pártos, Gy. 1985. "Linkages of the Light Industry." *Figyelő*, no. 34 (H).

Rácz, M. 1985. "The Electronics Industry in Worse Conditions." *Figyelő*, no. 29 (H).

Révész, G. 1988. "The Distortion Process of Economic Reform." *Közgazdasági Szemle*, no. 6: 661–73 (H).

Rosati, D., and Mizsei, K. 1988. "Adjustment Through Opening of Socialist Economies." Paper prepared for the World Insitute for Development Economics Research (WIDER), Helsinki, Finland.

Soós, K.A. 1988. "The Role of Money in the Recession Phase of Socialist Cycles." *Tervgazdasági Fórum*, no. 1: 19–32 (H).

Szalai, E. 1988. "The Nature of the Economic Crisis." *Valóság*, no. 6: 51–65 (H).

Szamuely, L. 1982. "The First Wave of the Mechanism Reform Debate in Hungary 1954–57." *Acta Oeconomica*, no. 1–2: 1–24.

———. 1984. "The Second Wave of the Economic Mechanism Debate and the 1968 Reform in Hungary." *Acta Oeconomica*, no. 1–2: 43–67.

———. 1988. "Towards a Comprehensive Economic Reform?—A Pessi-Optimistic View." Paper presented at the Conference on The Challenge of Simultaneous Economic Relations with East and West, Bellagio, March, 1988.

Török, A. 1985. "Linkages of the Engineering Industry." *Figyelő*, no. 24 (H).

———. 1986. *Comparative Advantages. International Examples, Domestic Experience*. Budapest: KJK (H).

———. 1989. "Lobbies and Development Anomalies in the Hungarian Microeletronic-Components Industry." *Közgazdasági Szemle*, no. 12 (H).

———. 1990. "Currency Conversion in the 'Two-Market' Foreign Trade." *Külgazdaság*, December (H).

———. 1992. "Egy vagyoncsökkentô vállalat a magyar elektronikai iparban" (An asset-subtracting firm in the Hungarian electronics industry). *Közgazdasági Szemle*, no. 1: 46–58.

———, ed. 1991. "Market Orientation—EC Integration." Research report prepared in the framework of the ACE Programme of the European Communities by the Research Institute of Industrial Economics of the Hungarian Academy of Sciences, Budapest, 1991.

Vissi, F. 1988. "Economic Policy Questions of Competition and of Market." *Tervgazdasági Fórum*, no. 2: 9–23 (H).

Wass von Czege, A. 1987. "Hungary's 'New Economic Mechanism': Upheaval or Continuity?" In *Crisis and Reform in Socialist Economies*, ed. Peter Gey, Jiří Kosta, and Wolfgang Quaisser. Boulder, CO: Westview Press, pp. 121–44.

Index